WOLSELEY
RADIAL
AERO ENGINES

Lord Nuffield's
Thwarted Venture

WOLSELEY RADIAL AERO ENGINES

Lord Nuffield's Thwarted Venture

PETER SEYMOUR

TEMPUS

First published 2006

Tempus Publishing Limited
The Mill, Brimscombe Port,
Stroud, Gloucestershire, GL5 2QG
www.tempus-publishing.com

British Library Cataloguing in Publication Data.
A catalogue record for this book is available from the British Library.

ISBN 0 7524 3915 4
  978 0 7524 3915 0

Typesetting and origination by Tempus Publishing Limited
Printed in Great Britain

CONTENTS

AUTHOR'S NOTE

William Richard Morris (1877–1963) was knighted in 1929. In 1934, he became a Baron, taking the name Lord Nuffield from a small village close to his home in Oxfordshire. It was in 1938 that he became a Viscount, but for simplicity the title of Lord Nuffield has been used throughout the main body of this account.

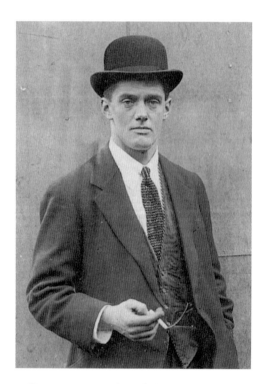

William Morris/Lord Nuffield.

ACKNOWLEDGEMENTS

In gathering information for this book, I have sought the co-operation of several people and organisations. My warmest thanks for their important contributions are, therefore, extended to:

Robin Barraclough
George Barton
Barry Blight
John Burnett
Anthony Clare
Julian Collins
Bob Cook
Harry Edwards
Geoff Fishwick
Brian Folkard
Mick Jeffries
Roy Maddison
Chas Moody
Eric Moore
Roy Oswell
Norman Painting

Brian Riddle
Geoffrey Rose
Richard Warburton
Jonathan Wood
Bablake School, Coventry
Birmingham Central Library
The British Motor Industry Heritage Trust
The Civil Aviation Authority
The Institute of Mechanical Engineers
Jaguar Daimler Heritage Trust Ltd
Nuffield College, Oxford
The Royal Aeronautical Society
Royal Air Force Museum, Hendon
The Science Museum, London
Warwick University

Except where otherwise stated, all photographs and illustrations shown in this book are from the author's own collection.

INTRODUCTION

In just over thirty years from the start of his career in 1893, building bicycles, Lord Nuffield's enterprise was transformed into the largest vehicle manufacturer in Britain. He became well known both as a successful industrialist and for his vast charitable gifts; during his lifetime he gave away over £30 million.

Lord Nuffield was equally well known for the manufacture of Morris cars, his connection with the MG Marque and, to a lesser extent, for his connections with Wolseley, Riley, Morris-Commercial and the carburetter manufacturer S.U..

What is less well known is his interest in aviation which led him, in 1929, to enter the aero engine manufacturing business through one of his companies, Wolseley Motors Ltd.

Lord Nuffield.

Lord Nuffield's interest in taking up the manufacture of aero engines stemmed from his belief that the ownership of private aeroplanes would become almost as common as the ownership of private motor cars. Although of considerable interest, Lord Nuffield's aero engine venture in the 1930s was not successful and it contributed to a long-running dispute between Lord Nuffield and the Government over the Shadow Factory scheme.

In principle, Lord Nuffield's plan to manufacture a new range of aero engines was sound, but it was not easy trying to break into a market that was already dominated by several well-established aero engine builders during the period of the Great Depression. Furthermore, the 1930s saw an intense change in international politics, and while orchestrating a programme of rearmament, the Air Ministry decided that it should only work with those aero engine manufacturers whose products were already proven, so it showed little interest in companies such as Wolseley who were trying to enter the market with new products.

CHRONOLOGY 1837–1938

THE WOLSELEY SHEEP SHEARING MACHINE CO. LTD

1837   Frederick York Wolseley is born in Co. Dublin, Ireland.

1854   F.Y. Wolseley sails from Ireland to Australia.

1867   F.Y. Wolseley becomes manager of a sheep station in New South Wales, Australia.

1887   F.Y. Wolseley establishes the Wolseley Sheep Shearing Machine Co. in Sydney, Australia. Herbert Austin joins the company.

1889   F.Y. Wolseley sells the Wolseley Sheep Shearing Machine Co. and the new owners register another company in London, using the same name.

1892   Herbert Austin becomes manager of Wolseley's factory in Broad Street, Birmingham.

1895   The Wolseley Sheep Shearing Machine Co. moves to a larger factory in Alma Street, Birmingham. Herbert Austin begins to design a motor car.

1896   The first Wolseley car is exhibited at Crystal Palace, London.

1900   A Wolseley car successfully completes the Thousand Miles Trial around Britain and many orders are received for an improved model.

THE WOLSELEY TOOL & MOTOR CAR CO. LTD
AND WOLSELEY MOTORS LTD

1901   Vickers Sons & Maxim Ltd buys the motor manufacturing part of the Wolseley Sheep Shearing Machine Co.'s business and forms the Wolseley Tool & Motor Car Co. Herbert Austin is made manager.

1902   The Siddeley Autocar Co. is formed to manufacture Siddeley cars in a Vickers factory at Crayford, Kent.

1903   The first Siddeley car is exhibited at Crystal Palace, London.

1905   The Siddeley Autocar Co. is taken over by the Wolseley Tool & Motor Car Co. Herbert Austin resigns and J.D. Siddeley takes over his position as general manager.

1908   The first Wolseley aero engine is introduced.

1909   J.D. Siddeley resigns. A Voisin biplane becomes the first aircraft to be fitted with a Wolseley aero engine.

1914   The Wolseley Tool & Motor Car Co. Ltd is renamed Wolseley Motors Ltd. Wolseley achieves an annual production of over 3,000 cars and had become the largest British-owned vehicle manufacturer in the UK.

1914–1918   Wolseley manufacture Renault, Royal Aircraft Factory and Hispano-Suiza aero engines under licence.

1919   Wolseley create £1.7 million, 6.5 per cent debenture stock to finance an expansion programme.

1920   The post-war boom collapses and Wolseley begins to get into financial difficulties.

1926   Wolseley Motors Ltd becomes bankrupt.

WOLSELEY MOTORS (1927) LTD
AND WOLSELEY AERO ENGINES LTD

Jan. 1927   Lord Nuffield buys Wolseley Motors Ltd from the receivers.

Feb. 1927   Wolseley Motors Ltd becomes Wolseley Motors (1927) Ltd.

1928/29   Light aircraft are being sold in increasing numbers. Private flying becomes both popular and affordable.

July 1929   Lord Nuffield instructs Wolseley to start the design and manufacture of a range of radial aero engines to suit light aircraft.

Oct. 1929   The Wall Street Crash occurs in the USA and 'The Great Depression' looms.

1930   In Britain, unemployment soars and inflation rises due to the Depression. The market for privately owned light aircraft begins to collapse.

July 1931   Wolseley's prototype radial aero engine makes its first flight.

Sept. 1931   Britain comes off the Gold Standard and the pound loses almost a third of its value.

Sept. 1932   'The Great Depression' enters its third year. Sales of light aircraft are few and far between.

April 1933   Leonard Lord becomes the managing director of Morris Motors Ltd.

July 1933   The first of Wolseley's range of radial aero engines is announced when three Hawker Tomtits, fitted with Wolseley A.R.9. engines, take part in the King's Cup Air Race.

Nov. 1933   Wolseley promote their aero engines to the Air Ministry as the market for light aircraft has diminished, but receive a negative response.

1934   The British economy begins a slow recovery.

June 1934   The prototype Airspeed Envoy makes its maiden flight, powered by a pair of Wolseley aero engines.

June 1935   Wolseley Aero Engines Ltd is formed to take over the aero engine business from Wolseley Motors (1927) Ltd. Lord Swinton becomes the Air Minister. His task is to increase the size of the RAF.

July 1935   Lord Nuffield asks for an appointment to meet the Air Minister, Lord Swinton, but his request is refused. Morris Motors Ltd buys Wolseley Motors Ltd. The (1927) is dropped.

Nov. 1935   Lord Nuffield meets with members of the Air Ministry, but his offer of help in producing aero engines is turned down.

Mar. 1936   The Air Ministry ask seven motor manufacturers, including Wolseley Motors Ltd, to co-operate in a scheme to jointly manufacture Bristol aero engines.

Apr. 1936   The motor manufacturers agree to set up the Shadow Factory scheme to make Bristol aero engines and form an Aero-Engine Committee with Lord Austin as chairman.

May 1936 Lord Nuffield withdraws Wolseley from the Shadow Factory scheme. The Air Ministry turn down Lord Nuffield's offer for Wolseley to make complete Bristol aero engines.

July 1936 Lord Nuffield informs the Air Ministry that Wolseley will rejoin the Shadow Factory scheme if the Air Ministry buys a building from Morris Motors Ltd to use as a Shadow Factory, but the offer is declined.

Aug. 1936 Leonard Lord tells the Air Ministry that Wolseley will re-enter the Shadow Factory scheme and agrees for a Shadow factory to be built nearby to Wolseley's factory in Birmingham. Leonard Lord resigns. Wolseley Motors Ltd, once again, withdraws from the Shadow Factory Scheme. The Air Ministry order 300 Wolseley Scorpio aero engines but Lord Nuffield dislikes the terms of the contract. The factory operated by Wolseley Aero Engines Ltd is closed down, so the Scorpio engines are not supplied.

Oct. 1936 Lord Nuffield issues a statement to the Press about his disagreement with the Air Ministry over aero engine production. The Government is widely criticised and issues a White Paper. Parliament debates Lord Nuffield's disagreement with the Air Ministry.

1937 The British economy returns to stability. Unemployment falls sharply as business improves.

Sept. 1937 Wolseley Aero Engines Ltd is merged with Nuffield Mechanizations Ltd to form Nuffield Mechanizations & Aero Ltd.

May 1938 Lord Swinton, the Air Minister, resigns. The new Air Minister, Sir Kingsley Wood, invites Lord Nuffield to 10, Downing Street, London. Lord Nuffield agrees to establish a factory for the mass production of Spitfires.

THE EARLY HISTORY OF THE WOLSELEY CO.

Although they were pioneers in the manufacture of both cars and aero engines, the origins of the Wolseley company lay with the production of machinery for shearing sheep.

Frederick York Wolseley was born on 16 March 1837 at the sizable Goldern Bridge House, Kilmainham, Co. Dublin. Three years later, in 1840, his father, Garnet Joseph Wolseley, died leaving a family of seven children (one of whom was to become the renowned Sudan war hero, Field Marshall Viscount Wolseley) to be brought up by their mother in difficult circumstances.

At the age of seventeen, in July 1854, F.Y. Wolseley sailed from Ireland to Australia aboard an emigrant ship, the SS *Norwood*, and following an apprenticeship, he became the manager of the Warbreccan Sheep Station, near Deniliquin, New South Wales. After working at other sheep stations, Wolseley realised that manual sheep shears needed to be replaced by shears powered mechanically, as the population of sheep was increasing; so he began to develop his new idea in about 1868.

The urgency of the need for a mechanical device can be gauged from the fact that in 1792 the total number of sheep in Australia was 105, and in 1860 the number in New South Wales alone had risen to well over 6 million, increasing to 35 million in 1880.[1]

Following many experiments and costly setbacks, Wolseley was granted several patents for sheep shearing machines, and to exploit them, he formed the Wolseley Sheep Shearing Machine Co. Ltd in 1887, with offices in Sydney, Australia. One of the engineering firms which made parts for Wolseley's sheep shearing machinery was managed by Herbert Austin (1866–1941), whose involvement with this business was to lead him into playing a significant part in the British motor industry. Herbert Austin was born in Little Missenden, Buckinghamshire, but spent his early life in Wentworth, Yorkshire, where his father was a farm bailiff. Although Austin was encouraged to pursue an architectural career, owing to his artistic talent:

> … his growing interest in engineering resulted in his parents applying, on his behalf, for an apprenticeship with the Great Northern Railway. But before he could take it up, his mother's brother arrived from Australia and his tales of the antipodes so captivated the eighteen year old Herbert that he accompanied his uncle on his return there.[2]

On his arrival in Australia during 1884, Herbert Austin obtained a job with an engineering workshop in Melbourne, which was managed by his uncle for a Scotsman called Mephan Ferguson. Some two years later, Austin decided 'to get right away from domestic authority',[3] so he left his uncle's workshop and moved out of his home. He then joined another Melbourne firm enagaged in the importation and erection of Crossley gas engines and printing presses.

Above left: Frederick York Wolseley.

Above right: Herbert Austin, *c.*1901.

Next, Austin went to the Langlands Foundry Co., also in Melbourne, and although he had mixed feelings about the business, he later recalled that it was there he 'received a thorough training as a mechanic'.[4] After leaving Langlands Foundry, Austin became the manager of the small engineering firm that undertook work for the Wolseley Sheep Shearing Machine Co. and when he made several suggestions to improve the reliability of the mechanical sheep shears, which were proving to be troublesome, F.Y. Wolseley asked him to join his enterprise. On taking up this post, Austin spent some time working alongside operators in a shearing shed in order to observe the sheep shears whilst they were in use, and he evolved many ideas for further improving the machines which he later patented.

In August 1889, F.Y. Wolseley sold the Wolseley Sheep Shearing Machine Co. Ltd and the new owners then formed an additional company in London, which was registered on 9 October 1889, using the same name. Although metamorphosed through a number of activities since 1889, this business still exists and is now known as Wolseley plc who are distributors for plumbing and building materials.

Three months after selling his business, in November 1889, F.Y. Wolseley rejoined the firm and was elected as its managing director with the responsibility of looking after the company's business in both Australia and New Zealand but, owing to ill health, his contract was terminated in May 1894. Wolseley later traveled to England where he died on 8 January 1899 at the age of sixty-one, leaving an estate valued at a modest £115 and without seeing the many products and several firms which were to subsequently bear his name.

After being established in Britain, the Wolseley Sheep Shearing Machine Co. began the manufacture of sheep shears by employing sub-contractors, but when these shears were found to be defective, Wolseley's reputation suffered. To try and recover the situation, Herbert Austin returned to Britain in March 1892 and became responsible for visiting the sub-contractors to implement quality control. Having persevered for about ten months, Austin was given permission to equip a small factory in Broad Street, Birmingham, so that Wolseley could undertake the manufacture of the sheep shears themselves. Even so, Wolseley found it difficult to restore its reputation, despite an immediate improvement in the quality of the shears coupled with an advertising campaign, so the business was diversified into the manufacture of machine tools and parts for bicycles. Austin was then appointed as the 'Inspector of Machines and Works Manager for England' and, in return for assigning his own patents relating to sheep shears to the company, Austin was allotted forty fully paid-up £5 shares.

During October 1895, the company moved to a larger factory in Alma Street, Birmingham and, while managing this factory, Herbert Austin began the design of motor cars, having been impressed by the three-wheeled Bollee[4] type of vehicle. Although it has sometimes been suggested otherwise, recent research into the Board Minutes of the Wolseley Sheep Shearing Machine Co. Ltd has revealed that seven months later, in May 1896, Austin was given approval to embark on the construction of two Wolseley motor cars, at a cost of not more than £100 each. As a result, Austin commenced work on the first of the two Wolseley cars, a three-wheeler with a pair of tiller-steered front wheels and an exposed flat-twin engine, but this vehicle was not announced publicly until 1904. By then, the second Wolseley car had not only been completed but also shown at the National Cycle Exhibition which was held at the Crystal Palace, London, during December 1896. This car was another three-wheeler, but with a single, tiller-steered front wheel and a two-cylinder engine. However, the two-cylinder engine was later abandoned and the car was then developed with an engine having a single cylinder.

By July 1898, Herbert Austin had been authorised to work on four more cars and their development was such that two Wolseleys, powered by 3½hp and 8hp engines respectively, were entered into the famous Thousand Miles Trial around Britain, which took place during April and May 1900. As the 8hp vehicle was not ready in time for the start of the trial in London, it was entered two days later in Birmingham, but retired soon afterwards. Nevertheless, the 3½hp machine, a tiller-steered four-wheeler driven by Herbert Austin himself, completed the course and gained first prize in its class, together with other awards, thereby demonstrating its durability and reliability to the public. Soon after the trial, the Alma Street factory received a flood of orders for an improved model known as the 'Wolseley Voiturette'.

A view of Wolseley's first motor car. Although work began in 1895 on this car, which was powered by an exposed flat-twin engine of about 2hp mounted near the rear wheel, it was not announced publicly until 1904.

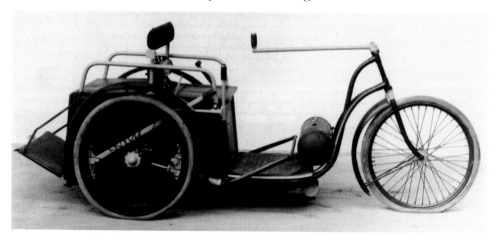

The second Wolseley motor car to be built. This car was first exhibited in December 1896.

Announced late in 1899, this is the first four-wheeled Wolseley motor car to be made. Driven by Herbert Austin, the tiller-steered, 3½hp vehicle competed in the Thousand Miles Trial around Britain of April/May 1900, in which it gained first prize in its class.

The directors of the Wolseley Sheep Shearing Machine Co. then decided to sell the motor manufacturing side of the operation in order to raise some finance. After negotiating with several organisations, the business was purchased by Vickers Sons & Maxim Ltd, a large armaments manufacturer, which then formed the Wolseley Tool & Motor Car Co. Ltd in February 1901, and appointed Herbert Austin as general manager.

The new company began its operations in a factory that Vickers had recently acquired at Adderley Park, Birmingham, and their first catalogue, which was issued on 1 May 1901, listed four Wolseley models in addition to a van with a detachable top. Due to high start-up costs, however, the company showed a loss in 1901, despite producing some 323 vehicles in that year, and although profits were made in 1902 and 1903, losses were again incurred during the following two years.

THE "WOLSELEY"

8 H.P. TONNEAU.

*Best Finish. Most Silent. Speedy.
Reliable.
The car that can be depended upon to do
all the work required of a car.*

Write for full particulars of

6 H.P., 8 H.P., 12 H.P., 16 H.P., 24 H.P. and 32 H.P.

"WOLSELEY" CARS

TO

The Wolseley Tool and Motor-Car Co., Ltd.,

**CRAYFORD,
KENT.** **Adderley Park,
Birmingham.**

This advertisement
appeared in March 1904.

In 1902, J.D. Siddeley (later Lord Kenilworth) approached Vickers with his own design of motor car, which he wished to have manufactured for himself. Instead of the horizontal type of engine that was being fitted to Wolseley cars, Siddeley proposed a vehicle with a vertical engine and, as this type of design was gaining in popularity, the directors of Vickers were eager to become involved. They agreed that Siddeley's design should be developed by Wolseley and that the car should be built at a factory in Crayford, Kent, which was already owned by Vickers. The Siddeley Autocar Co. was then registered and the first Siddeley cars were exhibited to the public in January 1903.

Being well received and gaining favourable technical reports, the demand for Siddeley cars soon exceeded expectations so, during the early part of 1905, Vickers instructed Wolseley to open negotiations with J.D. Siddeley and as a result his business was taken over by the Wolseley Tool & Motor Car Co. Siddeley was then appointed as Wolseley's sales manager but he only held this position for a few months as he was given the position of general manager in the summer of 1905, after Herbert Austin's resignation following several disputes over design and company policy. With some of Wolseley's senior staff whom he had taken with him, Herbert Austin then established the Austin Motor Co. Ltd at Longbridge, Birmingham, in December 1905 and the company later became one of Britain's major motor manufacturers.

During the 1906 season, Wolseley produced 523 cars which were a mixture of both 'Wolseley' and 'Siddeley', but in the following year all the models were named 'Siddeley'.

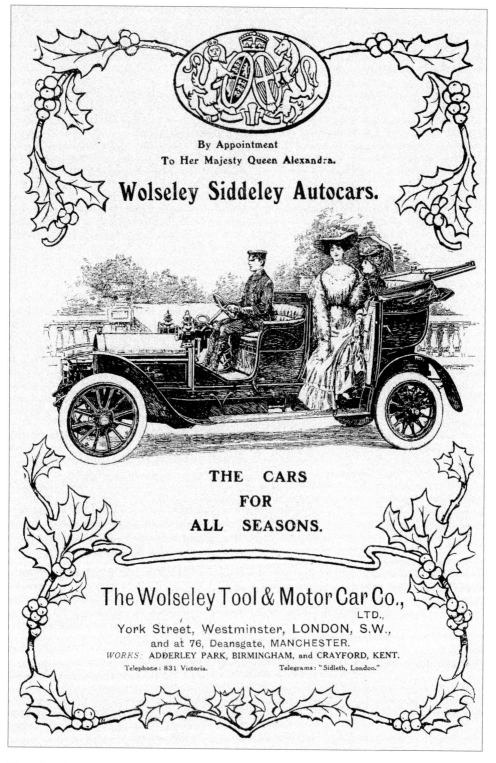

This advertisement appeared in December 1906.

Above left: J.D. Siddeley.

Above right: A 60hp Wolseley V8 marine engine which was advertised in 1912, for £500.

Despite the change of management, the Wolseley company continued to show financial losses and this situation eventually prompted Siddeley's resignation during the spring of 1909,[6] after which the name 'Siddeley' was dropped and 'Wolseley' was again used for the whole range of the company's vehicles. In order to reduce overheads and implement economies, Vickers reorganised Wolseley's manufacturing facilities and appointed Ernest Hopwood as managing director in July 1909. These events not only resulted in a rapid expansion of Wolseley's business, but the company also began to show a profit for the first time since 1903.

In 1904, while Herbert Austin had been managing the business, Wolseley started to manufacture a range of marine engines in addition to making motor cars. They also made some horizontal, sixteen-cylinder engines for submarines as well as engines for rail cars. The company first turned its attention to the design of aero engines in 1907, and a 30hp, water-cooled, vertical four-cylinder unit, with a capacity of 3.98 litres, appeared in 1908. However, as this engine proved to have insufficient power for its purpose, it was followed soon afterwards by a 50hp V8, effectively a double version four-cylinder unit. When this V8 was installed into a Voisin biplane, it became the first Wolseley engine to power an aircraft which, in the hands of M. de Baeder, was successful in winning four prizes on 30 December 1909. These prizes were the Prix des Pilots, the Prix des Arts et Metiers, the Coupe Archdeacon and the Prix Capitaine Berger. The first two were won by a flight of 3km, while the Archdeacon Cup was secured with a trip of 8.2km, beating the old record by 6.5km. The last prize was won by rising to a height of more than 100m, the actual altitude being 107m.[7]

Above, inset: In 1909, this Voisin biplane became the first aircraft to be powered by a Wolseley aero engine.

Above: M. de Beader inspecting the Wolseley V8, 50hp engine fitted to his Voisin biplane.

This advertisement appeared in January 1910.

WOLSELEY AERO ENGINES MANUFACTURED PRIOR TO 1915

The published data for Wolseley aero engines manufactured prior to 1915 is often contradictory. The figures in the following tables are taken from what appears to be the most reliable source.

WOLSELEY AERO ENGINES AVAILABLE IN 1908, 1909 AND 1910

HP	RPM	Max. BHP for short periods	No. of cyls. & arrangement	Bore & Stroke inches	Capacity litres	Cooling	Approx. weight lb
30	1100	35.3	4 in-line	3¾ x 5½	3.98	water	242
50	1350	60.4	90° Vee	3¾ x 5	7.24	water	340

Notes concerning the 50hp engine

1) The engine, which was priced at £600, was so constructed that the propeller could be driven as follows:
   - a) coupled direct to the crankshaft; in this condition the flywheel could be dispensed with and the weight reduced to 320lb.
   - b) coupled to the camshaft, giving a ratio of 0.5:1.
   - c) via gears and chains wheels, to drive a pair of contra-rotating propellers.
2) To simulate the conditions of actual flight, engines were tested by mounting them onto motor car chassis, complete with radiator and a fan brake. With an engine running at full power, the car was then driven over rough roads at 20 to 30mph for three to four hours.

WOLSELEY AERO ENGINES AVAILABLE IN 1911 AND 1912

HP	RPM	Max. BHP for short periods	No. of cyls & arrangement	Bore & Stroke inches	Capacity litres	Cooling	Approx. weight lb
60	1200	75	8.90° Vee	3¾ x 5½	7.96	water	300
120	1150	140	8.90° Vee	5 x 7	18.02	water	580

Notes

1) Overhead valve arrangement:
  60hp engine; automatic (atmospheric) inlet. Mechanical exhaust.
  120hp engine; the inlet and exhaust valves on each cylinder are mechanically operated by a single push rod and a single rocker.
2) The weights of 300lb and 580lb, for the 60hp and 120hp engines respectively, are complete with magneto, wiring, plugs, all water pipes on engine, water pump, oil pump, piping and connections but exclusive of flywheel, exhaust pipes and radiator. The 120hp engine weighs 695lb complete with accessories and the same engine weighs 805lb complete with accessories, radiator and coolant.

WOLSELEY AERO ENGINES AVAILABLE IN 1913 AND 1914

HP	RPM	Max. BHP for short period	No. of cyls & arrangement	Bore & Stroke inches	Capacity litres	Cooling	Approx. weight lb
75	1800	–	8.90° Vee	3¾ x 5½	7.96	air/water	380
90	1800	–	8.90° Vee	4 x 5½	9.06	water	405
130	1200	150	8.90° Vee	5 x 7	18.02	water	720

Notes

1) 75hp engine; air cooled with water-cooled exhaust valves.
2) 75 and 90hp engines; camshaft runs in roller bearings and is fitted with a ball thrust bearing to take propeller drive, giving a ratio of 0.5:1.
3) The weights quoted for the engines are complete with accessories.

General information

1) Engines were guaranteed to maintain their specific hp at their specified rpm for four hours.
2) The method of taking the drive for the propeller from an engine's camshaft is described in Wolseley's patent No.6038, which was accepted on 13 January 1910.
3) The arrangement for an air-cooled engine with water-cooled exhaust valves is described in Wolseley's patent No.18168, which was accepted on 7 August 1917.

By 1914, when the company had become the largest British-owned motor manufacturer in Great Britain, Wolseley employed some 4,000 staff and had achieved a production of over 3,000 cars per annum. This was in addition to a number of purpose-built commercial vehicles which had been introduced at the end of 1912, as well as aero, marine and other types of engines. To reflect all this, and to be more concise, the name of the company was changed, in July 1914, from the Wolseley Tool & Motor Car Co. Ltd to Wolseley Motors Ltd.

  Within a few days of the start of the First World War, Wolseley were asked to undertake the manufacture of aero engines, although the Government could supply neither drawings nor samples of the engines they required. Nevertheless, the first engines were on test eleven weeks after the request while the first deliveries were made a week later. The number of aero engines being delivered by Wolseley to the Government grew rapidly throughout the course of the war, during which the company manufactured Renault and

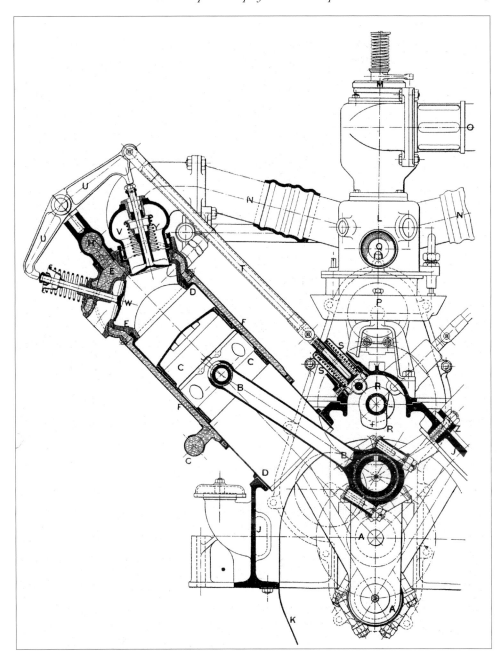

A sectioned view of the 120hp Wolseley V8 engine, showing the inlet and exhaust valves operated by a single push rod and a single rocker.

RAF (Royal Aircraft Factory, later known as the Royal Aircraft Establishment) air-cooled engines. Wolseley also built the advanced V8 Hispano-Suiza water-cooled aero engines, under licence; these engines were named the Python, Viper and Adder, which were fitted to several types of British fighter planes. By the end of the war, the company had produced nearly 3,000 aero engines (as shown in the table on page 28) in addition to some 700 complete aircraft, as well as propellers, armoured cars, army lorries, staff cars, ambulances, gun mountings, gun sights, shells and other munitions.

A 1913/14 Wolseley 30cwt van based on a type CP chassis. The vehicle is pictured on the forecourt of the East Works part of Wolseley's factory at Adderley Park, Birmingham, with the two-storey main office building of West Works in the background.

WOLSELEY-RENAULT AERO ENGINES MANUFACTURED BETWEEN 1914 AND 1918

Type	No. of cyls & arrangement	Cooling	Bore/stroke m/m	Litres capacity	Nominal hp	BHP	Normal rpm	Approx. weight lb
WB/WC tractor	8. 90° Vee	Air	96 x 120	6.94	70	76	1800	440

Applications: RAF BE 2, 2a, b,c, d, e, f, g., Airco DH 1, Armstrong Whitworth FK 2, Blackburn type E, Caudron G 111, Central Centaur IVA, Maurice Farman Serie II, Flanders F4, White & Thompson 'Bognor Bloater'.

Type	No. of cyls & arrangement	Cooling	Bore/stroke m/m	Litres capacity	Nominal hp	BHP	Normal rpm	Approx. weight lb
WB/WC pusher with cooling fan	8. 90° Vee	Air	96 x 120	6.94	70	72	1800	490
WX	8. 90° Vee	Air	100 x 120	7.54	75	85	1800	455
WS Tractor	8. 90° Vee	Air	105 x 130	9.01	80	105	1800	480

Applications: RAF S.E.5a, Airco DH6, Alliance P 1, Avro 548, Cuardron G III, Maurice Farman Serie II & VII, Vickers FB 7A.

Type	No. of cyls & arrangement	Cooling	Bore/stroke m/m	Litres capacity	Nominal hp	BHP	Normal rpm	Approx. weight lb
WS pusher with cooling fan	8. 90° Vee	Air	105 x 130	9.01	80	98	1800	520

WOLSELEY-ROYAL AIRCRAFT FACTORY AERO ENGINES MANUFACTURED 1916 – 1917

Type	No. of cyls & arrangement	Cooling	Bore & Stroke inches	Capacity litres	Cooling	Approx weight lb
RAF 1.a	8.90° Vee	Air	100 x 140	8.8	90	450

Applications: RAF BE 2c, d, e. BE 9. SE 5., Armstrong Whitworth FK 2, FK 3, Airco DH 6, Boulton Paul P 6 & P 9, de Havilland DH 51

Type	No. of cyls & arrangement	Cooling	Bore & Stroke inches	Capacity litres	Cooling	Approx weight lb
RAF 1.b.	8.90° Vee	Air	105 x 140	9.7	105	–

Applications: RAF BE 2e, Armstrong Whitworth FK 3.

WOLSELEY-HISPANO-SUIZA AERO ENGINES MANUFACTURED IN 1917 AND 1918

Type.	No. of cyls & arangement	Cooling	Bore/ Stroke mm	Litres capacity	Rated HP	Normal RPM	Comp. ratio	Approx. weight lb
Python I, W.4.A	8.90° Vee	Water	120 x 130	11.76	150	1500	4.7:1	455

Applications: RAF SE 5 & SE 5a., SPAD 7,

Type.	No. of cyls & arangement	Cooling	Bore/ Stroke mm	Litres capacity	Rated HP	Normal RPM	Comp. ratio	Approx. weight lb
Python II, W.4.A	8.90° Vee	Water	120 x 130	11.76	180	1800	5.3:1	465

Applications: RAF SE 5 & SE 5a, SPAD 7.

Type.	No. of cyls & arangement	Cooling	Bore/ Stroke mm	Litres capacity	Rated HP	Normal RPM	Comp. ratio	Approx. weight lb
Viper, W.4.A★	8.90° Vee	Water	120 x 130	11.76	210	–	–	–

Applications: Airco DH9. Avro 552, Bristol 13 M.R.1 & 88, Cierva C.8V, Martinside F 6, RAF SE 5 & SE 5a, Sopwith Cuckoo 7 Antelope

Type.	No. of cyls & arangement	Cooling	Bore/ Stroke mm	Litres capacity	Rated HP	Normal RPM	Comp. ratio	Approx. weight lb
Adder I & II, W.4 B	8.90° Vee	Water	120 x 130	11.76	200	2000	4.8:1	560

Applications: RAF SE 5 & SE 5a

Type.	No. of cyls & arangement	Cooling	Bore/ Stroke mm	Litres capacity	Rated HP	Normal RPM	Comp. ratio	Approx. weight lb
Adder III, W.4.B★	8.90° Vee	Water	120 x 130	11.76	200	2000	4:1	570

Applications: RAF SE 5 & SE 5a

Note

Weights are for complete engines with airscrew hubs.

AERO ENGINES DELIVERED BY WOLSELEY MOTORS LTD
1914 – 1918

Type	1914	1915	1916	1917	1918	Total delivered Aug. 1914 to Dec. 1918
Renault 70hp	4	96				100
Renault 80hp		16	283	4	1	304
R.A.F. 1a			150			150
R.A.F. 1b			14	35		49
Hispano-Suiza/150/180hp				224	1,629	1,853
Hispano-Suiza 200hp				445	4	449
A.B.C. Dragonfly					1	1
TOTALS	4	112	447	708	1635	2,906

These pages: Four views taken at Wolseley's Adderley Park factory in Birmingham, during the First World War.

Left: Machining aluminium parts for Wolseley aero engines.

Below: Aero engine test beds, enclosed by torpedo netting.

Installing engines into aircraft.

Royal Aircraft Factory, S.E.5a. fighters, fitted with Wolseley Viper engines, undergoing construction.

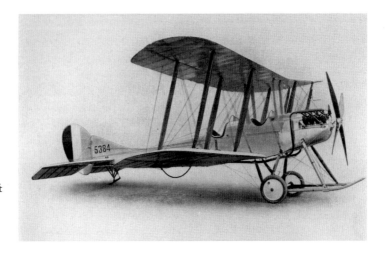

A Royal Aircraft Factory, B.E.2c. aircraft fitted with a 70hp Wolseley-Renault engine.

With abundant optimism for a boom in business after the First World War, and encouraged by good profits since 1909, Vickers decided that Wolseley should expand its production facilities. To accomplish this, Vickers sold Wolseley another factory at Drews Lane, in the Ward End district of Birmingham, even though their factory at Adderley Park had been greatly enlarged before and during the war. The extensive Ward End factory (now occupied by LDV Vans) had been built during 1914 for another Vickers subsidiary, the Electric & Ordnance Accessories Co. Ltd, to produce fuses and shell cases. Wolseley also decided to build a prestigious new showroom in Piccadilly, London, at a cost of nearly £250,000 (about £7½ million at 2006 values), for the display of the company's products. These ambitious developments were financed by the creation of £1.7 million (about £50 million at 2006 values) 6.5 per cent Debenture Stock in November 1919 but, when the post-war boom collapsed at the end of 1920 and the demand for vehicles declined sharply, Wolseley Motors Ltd began to get into financial difficulties as it had burdened itself with increased overheads and vast debt repayments. The situation deteriorated steadily and by the end of 1925, Wolseley had suffered successive losses totalling over £1 million.

Owing to Wolseley's difficulties, the Debenture Stock Holders held a meeting, on 28 September 1926, to seek a moratorium of three months, which was granted. A month later, on 26 October 1926, a creditor obtained judgement for £446 10s 0d, although this was withdrawn three days later on the appointment of the joint receivers and managers, Sir Gilbert Garnsey and Mr T.W. Horton. However, when the creditor re-presented the petition, on 1 November 1926, a winding-up order was made which resulted in Wolseley Motors Ltd being declared bankrupt with liabilities of over £2 million (about £78 million at 2006 values). The receivers then announced that the business would be sold by private auction, as a going concern.

At a meeting of Wolseley's creditors on 21 January 1927, the senior official receiver, Mr H.E. Burgess, outlined the company's financial position since 1901 and said:

> The losses sustained by [Wolseley Motors Ltd] from 1920 to 1925, and which amounted to £1,099,391, were attributed to the moulders' strike, [the] general trade depression in 1920–21, labour disputes in 1922 [and] heavy writing down of stocks in 1923, [together with a] reduction in prices of cars to meet severe competition, and further writing down of stocks values in 1925. During the same period the company redeemed £228,500 debenture stock at 105 per cent, at a cost of £239,925, and paid interest amounting to £601,575 on outstanding stock. I have come to the conclusion that the losses would have been materially less if the company only had the pluck to realise the position in 1922 when they should have consulted the debenture stockholders and made some scheme for reorganisation. It is also the case that the company suffered immensely by the issue of debentures instead of shares.

Mr Burgess ended his statement by saying:

> The failure of the company was attributed by its officials to the causes, previously given, for the losses [incurred] between 1920 and 1925, but it also appeared to be due to bad management, excessive factory charges, and the fact that the design of the company's production was unsuitable to public requirements.[8]

Wolseley's assets, coupled with its fine reputation, meant that the business was of interest to other motor manufacturers and offers were received from Lord Nuffield and Sir Herbert Austin,[9] as he had now become, who also wished to buy the company for sentimental reasons because of his previous connection with it. A third offer was tendered by Julius Turner, a thirty-year-old London financier who was said to be acting on behalf of a foreign

This advertisement appeared in April 1923.

company. It was later reported that Julius Turner had been representing the General Motors Corporation of America who were, at the time, looking for a manufacturing plant in England, but Lord Nuffield's biographers had no evidence of this.[10] Furthermore, Miles Thomas, who had worked for Lord Nuffield since 1924 and who was involved with his negotiations to purchase Wolseley, had a hunch that Julius Turner was, 'a speculator who, if he had obtained control, could have resold at an inflated price to Morris, to Austin or to some American company'.[11]

An aerial view of Wolseley's factory in the Ward End district of Birmingham, *c.*1938. If it had come to fruition, the Shadow Factory for the production of Bristol aero engines would have been built on the vacant land to the left of Drews Lane, which is seen running down the right-hand side of the picture.

An aerial view of Wolseley's Adderley Park factory in Birmingham, which was acquired by Lord Nuffield in 1927 and then occupied by Morris Commercial Cars Ltd from 1929. The East Works part of the factory, shown on the right of the picture, was separated from West Works by Bordesley Green Road. Some two thirds of the buildings of East Works were destroyed by fire on 5 May 1962 while those of West Works were demolished during the late 1970s. The entire site has since been redeveloped.

Lord Nuffield had a variety of reasons for wishing to purchase Wolseley Motors Ltd:

> … in the first place, he had no intention of letting the company go to a foreigner; secondly, since the time when he had been a Wolseley dealer, he had had a high regard for its product and was at this time particularly impressed by the Wolseley "Silent-Six",… [Before he had started the manufacture of motor vehicles, Lord Nuffield's garage business in Oxford, known as the 'Morris Garage', held several agencies including Wolseley.] Thirdly, Wolseley were known to have extensive, modern, and integrated plant; fourthly, the company would help him extend the range of his products into the higher price class, since besides the reputation of its products, it had a very good chain of distributors. Beyond these particular reasons [Lord Nuffield] was, at that time, interested in having companies which would to some extent compete with one another. With Wolseley he would get a first-class designing staff to give him an alternative to Cowley… and its engine and component production also provided a check on Morris Engines and other suppliers.[12]

After Lord Nuffield had been given permission to amend his initial offer of £600,000 for Wolseley Motors Ltd, despite the expiry of the time limit, Julius Turner disputed the right of the receivers to accept this arrangement. On 10 February 1927, the dispute was taken to the Law Courts in Carey Street, London, where the Master of the Court rejected the submission that Julius Turner's bid, which was higher than Lord Nuffield's initial offer, should be accepted. As a result, Julius Turner withdrew from the proceedings and an auction then started in the court when, having received permission, Lord Nuffield and Sir Herbert Austin bid verbally against each other. Being determined to buy Wolseley, Lord Nuffield outstripped each of Austin's bids and, at one point, Ernest Payton, Austin's financial director, privately asked him how far he intended to go to which he replied characteristically, 'I am going just a bit further than you'.[13] Lord Nuffield acquired Wolseley Motors Ltd when his bid for £730,000 (about £28 million at 2006 values) was unanswered. Commenting on the auction as he left the court, Lord Nuffield said, 'It was the most thrilling hour of my life'.[14] The company was then renamed Wolseley Motors (1927) Ltd, and it remained in Lord Nuffield's personal ownership until July 1935, when it was sold to Morris Motors Ltd.

At the time of the auction, Lord Nuffield's financial situation was very healthy as his sale of Preference Shares in Morris Motors Ltd, in 1926, had raised over £2¾ million (about £106 million at 2006 values). In addition to buying two factories located in the heart of the industrial Midlands, Lord Nuffield had also acquired an experienced workforce, amongst whom was Oliver Boden, Wolseley's much respected works manager, who became his deputy less than ten years later.

James Woodcock, who was an apprentice at Wolseley when the company changed hands and who also became Lord Nuffield's deputy during the 1950s, said of the takeover:

> There was great relief. Thank God something had happened to us. The old owners had had their yachts and their engines in for repair and servicing, and allowed [the company] to go bankrupt. My first sight of [Lord Nuffield] was when he had just bought [the business], seeing him walk along what they called the old mill with Oliver Boden, in his bowler hat and dirty old mac walking through, chin jutting out as I got to know so very well…[15]

Having spent a great deal of money on a loss-making company, employing some 1,200 people, Lord Nuffield then had the task of turning Wolseley into a profitable enterprise. During July 1927, Lord Nuffield appointed William Cannell as managing director of Wolseley Motors (1927) Ltd, having transferred him from Morris Commercial Cars Ltd where he had held a similar position, and adopted the title governing director for himself. (Prior to joining Morris Commercial Cars Ltd William Cannell had been the general manager of Gwynnes Ltd, a business involved in the manufacture of aero engines, cars

THE 11.22 h.p. Wolseley Saloon costs but £300 ; the 4-seater £215. For this you buy a car made in a British factory long famous for the production of high-grade motor carriages—a tradition that is fully maintained in this small model. Examine closely one of these cars. Note the shaft-driven overhead camshaft ; the accessible right hand brake and gear change ; the general sturdiness and mechanical perfection of the whole car. Then you will appreciate the wonderful value of the 11.22 Wolseley.

Don't buy any car until you have seen the 11.22 Wolseley Catalogue. It will be sent free on request.

11·22 h.p.

WOLSELEY

from £215

Wolseley Motors (1927) Ltd., Adderley Pk., Birmingham

This advertisement appeared in June 1927, five months after Lord Nuffield had purchased Wolseley Motors Ltd.

Above: Oliver Boden OBE.

Right: William Cannell (left) shaking hands with King George V.

and pumps.) At about the same time Leonard Lord, then aged thirty-one, was transferred to the Ward End factory to reorganise its machine shops. Recognised as a 'brilliant exponent of flow production methods',[16] Leonard Lord had previously been responsible for the design and purchase of machinery at Morris Engines Ltd, Coventry, where engines and gearboxes were being made with state-of-the-art, mass-production techniques. With his tough, unyielding and, sometimes, blunt manner, Leonard Lord soon made his presence felt at Wolseley when both he and Oliver Boden set about improving the company's situation.

As the total area provided by Wolseley's two factories was in excess of the company's requirements, it was decided to consolidate the business on to the Ward End factory[17] and, at the same time, dispose of some unprofitable sidelines. By the end of 1929, Wolseley's Adderley Park factory had been vacated and this factory became the home of Morris Commercial Cars Ltd after the company had transferred the manufacture of commercial vehicles from its original premises at Soho, Birmingham.

To provide financial support and working capital for the newly purchased business, Morris Industries Ltd, a holding company for Lord Nuffield's personal investments, loaned Wolseley a total of £195,000 (about £7½ million at 2006 values) between September 1927 and March 1929. These loans were repaid by Wolseley in April 1931 and during the early part of 1932, thereby indicating that it had apparently taken the company's new management just over four years to generate the necessary cash flow for the loans to be reimbursed.

Notes

1   Nixon, St John C., pp.13–14.

2   Wood, Jonathan, *Wheels of Fortune*, p.4.

3   *The Autocar*, 23 August 1929, p.371.

4   Ibid.

5   Leon Bollee was a good friend of Wilbur Wright, who succeeded with his brother Orville in making the first flight in a heavier-than-air machine in December 1903. In 1908, Leon Bollee provided Wilbur Wright with factory space for the assembly of the Wright 'A' Flyer with which Wilbur made the dramatic demonstration flights starting on 8 August 1908. Many years later, in 1924, Lord Nuffield purchased the assets and factory of Automobiles Leon Bollee, at Le Mans, France. The firm then made vehicles known as 'Morris Leon Bollee' until 1931, when the business was sold.

6   After he left Wolseley, J.D. Siddeley (1866–1953) became the general manager of The Deasy Motor Car Manufacturing Co., in Coventry, and was soon appointed managing director. In 1911 the company became known as the Siddeley-Deasy Motor Car Co., and it received its first contract to make aero engines in 1915. The Siddeley-Deasy Motor Car Co. sold their works to an armament firm, Armstrong Whitworth, in 1919, and the business was renamed Armstrong-Siddeley Motors Ltd in 1927. This company made aero engines, cars and aircraft and it joined with Hawker Aircraft to form Hawker Siddeley in 1935.

7   See *Flight*, 8 January 1910.

8   *The Garage and Motor Agent*, 29 January 1927, p.572.

9   Herbert Austin had been knighted in 1917 by King George V in recognition of his sevices to the country during the First World War when the production facilities of the Austin Motor Co., at Longbridge, were greatly increased in size to cope with orders for military vehicles, ambulances, aircraft, aero engines and other munitions.

10 Andrews & Brunner, p.155 n.

11 Thomas, Sir Miles, p.161.

12 Andrews & Brunner, p.155.

13 Andrews & Brunner, p.156.

14 Jackson, Robert, p.114.

15 Adeney, Martin, p.99.

16 Thomas, Sir Miles, p.165.

17 The factory at Ward End continued to manufacture Wolseley vehicles until 1949, when their production was moved to Morris Motors' plant at Cowley. The Ward End factory was then renamed Morris Motors Ltd, Tractor & Transmissions Branch.

2

THE ORIGINS OF WOLSELEY
RADIAL AERO ENGINES

Despite the fact that the first Morris car had only appeared in 1913, the popularity of the marque had increased to such an extent that by 1925 over 1,000 'Bullnose' Morris Cowleys and Oxfords were being manufactured and sold by Morris Motors Ltd each week, such that the company captured 41 per cent of all the new car sales in Britain during that year. Although privately owned aircraft were virtually non-existent before 1925, it was expected that one day members of the public would buy light aircraft for personal use in much the same way as they were already buying motor cars, and this situation was inevitably recognised by Lord Nuffield.

At the beginning of 1925, when it first became available, the de Havilland Moth biplane was priced at £885 and advertised 'for the school, the flying club and the private owner'. Its abilities were soon to be exhibited when Alan Cobham flew from Britain to Switzerland and back in one day, at an average speed of 71mph throughout. Taking off from Croydon Aerodrome at 4.54 a.m. on 29 May 1925, in the prototype Moth, G-EBKT, fitted with extra fuel tanks, Cobham arrived in Zurich just over 6 hours later having flown non-stop. Owing to a stiff head wind, the journey back to Croydon took 1¾ hours longer but a comparable journey by rail and sea would have taken 37 hours and would have cost £11, nearly two and a half times the price of the fuel and oil used by the Moth for its return journey. At the time it was deemed that, 'the importance of this flight lies in the fact that it has demonstrated the real possibilities of the light 'plane in a practical way, and has shown that it is possible for the "man-in-the-street" to fly – not merely short flights in or around an aerodrome, but comparatively long distances to foreign countries – with ease, safety and at reasonable cost...'[1] Personal air travel had, in the view of some, arrived at a price that many could afford.

To encourage private flying, the Government introduced a scheme to subsidise the operations of five Light Aeroplane Clubs during the summer of 1925. Initially, the scheme provided each club with two de Havilland Moths, a spare engine and sundry items, up to the value of £2,000, together with an assurance that half the cost of replacing a damaged aircraft would be met. In addition, each flying club received a grant of £1,000 for the first year to cover expenses, and a payment of £10 for each pilot's licence obtained after training on club aircraft. (Information on the Government Subsidised Light Aeroplane Clubs appears in Appendix 8.)

Although they had struggled through a difficult early period on their subscriptions and the allowance from the Treasury, the number of Government-subsidised Light Aeroplane Clubs had increased to six at the beginning of 1927, with a total membership of over 1,000. The clubs often staged air pageants to arouse public interest in flying and, as the sight of an aircraft at close quarters or in the air was still a novelty, the pageants usually attracted large

A 1925 Season 'Bullnose' Morris Cowley two seater, seen parked near to the foundry at Morris Motors' Cowley factory.

A de Havilland Moth being towed by a 1921 Season 'Bullnose' Morris Cowley four seater.

crowds of people. Another purpose of the pageants was to raise money by charging admission fees so that, together with donations from members and philanthropists, the Light Aeroplane Clubs could acquire new aircraft. Private flying was also being demonstrated by ex-service pilots who toured the country with their aircraft and offered joyrides to members of the public. For example, Surrey Flying Services, who advertised themselves in 1926 as 'The World's Premier Joyriders', charged 5s a head for a circuit and an additional 5s for looping the loop.

By the end of 1927, when it had a 43 per cent share of all private aircraft held on the Air Ministry's register, the de Havilland Moth had had its price reduced to £730 owing to the economies created by an increased level of production. The popularity of the Moth led to it being dubbed 'the motor car of the air' and in 1928 its price, with full equipment, painted any colours, registered and with a Government Certificate of Airworthiness, had fallen to £650. In comparison, a top of the range Morris Six Saloon could be purchased new, at that time, for £395. Along with other makes of light aircraft, the Moth combined the flexibility and convenience of a motor car with the benefit of speed. To share the cost of purchasing and operating a light aircraft, individuals sometimes formed syndicates of four or five persons. (See Appendix 10 for a list of 'Notable British Manufacturers of Light Aircraft in 1929'.)

The growth in the number of privately owned aircraft was such that, by the end of 1928, a total of 125 had been registered in addition to a further 125 aircraft that were being used for joyriding, air-taxi and miscellaneous work as well as by the Government-subsidised Light Aeroplane Clubs, which now numbered thirteen with a total membership of 3,288. With an interest in the developing market for light aircraft, Lord Nuffield visited the British Aircraft Show at Olympia, London, during July 1929 and, while inspecting the exhibits, he commented on the excessive cost of the aero engines. Lord Nuffield was reputed to have said that his organization could manufacture aero engines that would weigh no more than 1lb per horsepower and would cost £1 per horsepower but, according to *Flight* of 2 June 1938, 'Lord Nuffield never made these claims himself; they were wished upon him by doubtless well-meaning but ill-advised enthusiasts'. (Details of the aero engines on display at the British Aircraft Show in July 1929, appear in Appendix 2.)

Soon after the show Lord Nuffield gave the management at Wolseley Motors (1927) Ltd an instruction to develop, manufacture and market a range of air-cooled radial aero engines for light aircraft, to exploit an apparent business opportunity, thereby reviving Wolseley's involvement in aviation. Such instructions could be issued quickly and without the need of agreement from a board of directors, because Lord Nuffield personally owned the Wolseley company and, therefore, had sole control of the business.

Following this directive, an aero engine department was set up at Wolseley's Ward End factory which was entirely separate from the business of making motor cars and accessible only with an official pass. The activities of the aero engine department fascinated the rest of the workforce and, although the aero engine personnel shared the works canteen, they generally kept themselves to themselves. Amongst the staff of some sixty people engaged in making aero engines was the previously mentioned James Woodcock, who was put in charge of engine production. On his appointment, he protested that he had never been near an aero engine in his life, to which Leonard Lord, by then Wolseley's works manager, replied, 'It's about bloody time you were!'.[2]

Whilst William Cannell was in overall charge of Wolseley's operations, being the company's managing director, the aero engine department was under the control of Edward S. Luyks, a practical engineer who was already working as a designer for Wolseley Motors Ltd when Lord Nuffield had purchased the company. For the design of the new aero engines, Luyks was supported by Clifford O. Towler, who had joined Wolseley in 1929 from Armstrong-Siddeley Motors Ltd where he had been working as an aero engine designer since 1922. Some time later Donald Armour joined the design team from the Bristol Aeroplane Co. Ltd.

This photograph, which was probably taken in 1928, shows a de Havilland D.H.60G Gipsy Moth, registered G-AAAA, standing between two Morris cars. At that time, a new Gipsy Moth could be purchased for £650, 'ready to fly away', while the price of a new Morris Six Saloon was £395 and that of a Morris Six Coupe, shown on the left and right respectively, was £385. With Capt. Geoffrey de Havilland at the controls, G-AAAA set up a new two-seat light plane altitude record of 19,980ft on 28 July 1928.

This advertisement appeared in October 1928.

Edward S. Luyks.

The manufacture of aero engines called for the expansion of Wolseley's metallurgical department and expensive testing equipment was purchased to ensure that material specifications conformed to Air Ministry regulations. The department, which was to benefit the quality of the products being made by the entire Nuffield Organization, was under the control of H.S. (Spencer) Kipling who had taken up this appointment in 1910, when he was aged twenty-six. In addition to setting up a laboratory, Spencer Kipling also supervised the processes within the company's foundry, stamp shop and heat-treatment facilities.

Soon after being established, Wolseley's aero engine department had assembled its first engine which was then tested on a specially built test bed, creating a noise that could be heard throughout the factory. By February 1930 the level of progress within the department was such that Wolseley was able to invite Major George Bulman, the head of Engine Development at the Air Ministry, to visit the factory and to inspect a seven-cylinder radial engine that was under development. He found a 'workmanlike and interesting engine'[3] and, during a discussion with Mr Cannell and Mr Luyks, he explained the, 'current type-test schedule and special trials… which their engine would have to complete to secure a certificate of airworthiness'.[4] It was agreed that, like other firms who competed in the aero engine business, Wolseley should have assistance from the Ministry, if requested, so Wolseley's aero engine business had received an encouraging start.

It was in a report published on 1 November 1929 that *Flight* magazine first made an announcement to its readers concerning Lord Nuffield's intention to manufacture aero engines. The report added, 'It is not yet possible to disclose details but we hope to be able to do so later and in the meantime we feel the country can look to [Lord Nuffield] with gratitude for keeping us ahead of the foreshadowed cheap engine invasion from abroad.'

There was then a lapse of some ten months before *Flight* was able to provide brief details about Wolseley's aero engines when it said, in their issue of 5 September 1930:

> Last week, at Wolseley's Works, Birmingham, [Lord Nuffield] showed us privately the first of two types of engine which it is proposed to develop. The first, a seven cylinder radial, will shortly be submitted to the Air Ministry type test. The second engine is a nine cylinder radial. The new development is another indication of the enterprise and initiative of [Lord Nuffield] in the world of transport and engineering.

During May 1931, a Wolseley radial aero engine, almost certainly a seven-cylinder A.R.7 designated 'A.R.2', was ready to be installed into a Hawker Tomtit, G-ABOD, then owned by H.G. Hawker Engineering Co. Ltd. The designation 'A.R.2' appears in Hawker's test

Above: H.S. Kipling seated in the tiller steered Wolseley which competed in the famous Thousand Miles Trial of 1900. This picture was taken outside Block 'E' of Wolseley's factory in Ward End, Birmingham, at the time of Spencer Kipling's retirement in 1949, after he had completed thirty-nine years of service with the company. Also shown is an unregistered Wolseley Four-fifty saloon car.

Left: Major George P. Bulman of the Air Ministry.

Hawker Tomtit, G-ABOD, fitted with a Wolseley A.R.7. Aquarius, seven-cylinder radial aero engine. (The same aircraft, fitted with a Wolseley A.R.9, Aries, Mk II engine, is shown on p.48.)

flight data (see Appendix 5) and it is thought that this designation was allocated to identify the second engine built in the 'A.R.' series; the letters 'A.R.' are believed to stand for 'Air-cooled Radial'. Piloted by Flt-Lt P.G. Lucas, one of Hawker's test pilots, G-ABOD took off from Brooklands aerodrome on 24 July 1931 to make its first test flight under the power of a Wolseley aero engine, no doubt to the delight of Lord Nuffield.

Flt-Lt Philip Lucas had joined the H.G. Hawker Engineering Co. Ltd on 1 June 1931 and his log book shows that on 23 July 1931, he took off for a 30-minute flight as a passenger in G-ABOD when the aircraft was being piloted by Flt-Lt Bulman, Hawker's chief test pilot. However, as this flight is not recorded as an official test flight, it was probably a proving flight to gain experience with the new Wolseley 'A.R.2' engine. Subsequently, this engine was replaced by a nine-cylinder Wolseley A.R.9 and G-ABOD was first flown in this configuration by Flt-Lt P.E.G. Sayer on 1 September 1932. Details of the test flights undertaken by G-ABOD, powered by Wolseley engines, appear in Appendix 5.

Like many others, Lord Nuffield took a keen interest in the exploits of Amy Johnson and her achievement in being the first woman to make a solo flight from England to Australia. Flying a second-hand de Havilland D.H.60G Gipsy Moth named *Jason* and registered G-AAAH, Amy Johnson left Croydon Aerodrome on 5 May 1930 and arrived in Darwin to a heroine's welcome on 'Empire Day', 24 May, having flown some 10,000 miles. Among the many gifts presented to her in recognition of her epic journey that captured the headlines of the day was an M.G. 18/80, Mk I, Salonette car given by Lord Nuffield, in which, on 11 August 1930, she travelled to Buckingham Palace to receive the CBE from King George V.

In an article which appeared in the *Daily Chronicle* in January 1930, some four months before her journey, Amy Johnson, whose introduction to flying had been a 5s joyride with Surrey Flying Services, said:

You who fly; do tell your friends of the joys you experience in the air, of the exhilaration of knowing yourself free and alone in the glorious freedom of the skies, of the wonders to be seen… do you show them by your example as a fine, careful pilot, how safe it is to fly a machine so shining, clean and well cared for as your own? I hope you do. You will be helping to make Aviation History. You who would like to fly, but [have] no money.

Above: Standing with her parents, Amy Johnson is seen holding a door handle of the M.G. 18/80, Mk I, Salonette car which Lord Nuffield gave to her in recognition of being the first woman to make a solo flight from England to Australia. The mascot mounted on the car's radiator cap depicts Amy Johnson's de Havilland Gipsy Moth, *Jason.* (British Motor Industry Heritage Trust)

Left: This advertisement appeared in May 1930.

Flying is still pretty expensive because it is as yet a luxury for the minority instead of the pleasure of the majority. Think Aviation, Talk Aviation, Read Aviation, and if you're determined enough, your chance will come. I joined a Flying Club and had a half hour lesson per fortnight costing £1. I found I could save 10/- per week out of my typist's salary.

Being fiercely patriotic, Lord Nuffield wished to honour Amy Johnson personally but he also realised that her journey would promote the use of privately owned aircraft and thereby the sale of aero engines, although his commercial interest in aviation was not widely known at this time. This interest, however, was revealed to the public three years later, in July 1933, when Lord Nuffield entered three Hawker Tomtit aircraft into the King's Cup Air Race. These aircraft had been purchased by Wolseley in May 1933 to act as flying test beds and they were fitted with Wolseley, 185hp, A.R.9 engines. (A list of the thirty-five entrants in the 1933 King's Cup Air Race appears in Appendix 6.)

The Tomtits, which were registered G-ABAX, G-AASI and G-ABOD, were flown in the race by Flt-Lt P.W.S. (George) Bulman, George E. Lowdell and Flt-Lt P.E.G. (Gerry) Sayer, all of whom were experienced flyers. George Bulman was Hawker's chief test pilot, while George Lowdell, who had been a test pilot at RAF Martlesham Heath, was an instructor at Brooklands Flying School. A few months after the race, in February 1934, George Lowdell joined Wolseley as their chief test pilot and then carried out his duties from the Castle Bromwich aerodrome, near Birmingham. Gerry Sayer was also a test pilot and a member of George Bulman's team at the Hawker Co. During 1934, Gerry Sayer left Hawkers and joined the Gloster Aircraft Co. as their chief test pilot. On 15 May 1941 he made aviation history when he took off in the first British jet-propelled aircraft, the Gloster E28/39, on its maiden flight.

In an article about the 1933 King's Cup Air Race, *Flight* reported:

> The Tomtit flown by Sayer was examined with interest, because it was one of the three machines fitted with the new Wolseley A.R.9 engine. This particular machine [G-ABOD] had a direct- drive engine, while those flown by Bulman and Lowdell [G-ABAX and G-AASI] had geared engines. A very small wooden airscrew was fitted.[5]

During the race, which was divided into twelve heats and a final, the Tomtits flown by Sayer and Bulman were eliminated in heats four and nine respectively, both having being placed in sixth position in these heats. Of the three pilots, Lowdell was the most successful as his Tomtit reached the second heat of the semi-final (heat twelve) before being eliminated. Summarising the technical aspects of the race, which was won by Captain G. de Havilland in a Leopard Moth, *Flight* were of the opinion that the performance of the Wolseley A.R.9s, '…was a question of aircraft speeds and not of engine reliability'. 'In point of fact,' they continued, 'the three Wolseley [engines] sounded as if they would have enjoyed going the whole course.'[6]

Shortly after the race, which he had attended in person together with William Cannell and his adviser, Sqd. Ldr G.H. Reid,[7] Lord Nuffield explained his reasons for starting the manufacture of aero engines when he said:

> I have been considering the production of an aero engine for the last two or three years. There is no doubt that, as the aeroplane improves and becomes safer, so it will be more popular as a means of transport, and the more aeroplanes that are sold, the more reasonable their price will become. This also applies to the cost of the engines. I have no wish to build aeroplanes myself, and no intention of doing it, either. I am just out to sell engines to the manufacturers. There is no big demand for engines at the moment, but it was because we realised that the sale of aircraft would gradually climb – as did the sale of motor cars – that we decided it was time we set out to design engines for manufacturers. It might be true to say that the aeroplane is today

Lord Nuffield entered these Hawker Tomtits, fitted with Wolseley A.R.9. Aries engines, into the 1933 Kings Cup Air Race; the first time Wolseley radial aero engines had been seen in public. Shortly after the race, Lord Nuffield announced his intention to mass-produce aero engines for light aircraft. The same three aircraft were also entered into the 1934 Kings Cup Air Race. (*Flight*)

The Hawker Tomtit pilots who took part in the 1933 Kings Cup Air Race. From left to right: Flt-Lt P.E.G. Sayer (G-ABOD – racing No.8), Flt-Lt P.W.S. 'George' Bulman (G-ABAX, part of which is seen in the photograph – racing No.9) and George E. Lowdell (G-AASI – racing No.10). (*Flight*)

Lord Nuffield, left, standing with his adviser, Sqd-Ldr G.H. Reid, centre, and William Cannell, the managing director of Wolseley Motors (1927) Ltd, while attending the 1933 King's Cup Air Race.

where the motor car was in 1914. When aeroplanes are sold in sufficient quantities, there is no reason why they should not be as cheap as the light car today.[8]

Lord Nuffield was apparently convinced that he could mass produce aero engines for light aircraft at low cost, and thereby dominate the market in much the same way as he had with motor cars. With considerable foresight, he explained an additional reason for entering into the manufacture of aero engines when he said, 'I put up the aero engine factory because I realised that, in time of national emergency, firms with experience of building internal combustion engines might be called on for national defence, and I wished to play my part'.[9]

For the 1934 King's Cup Air Race, which was again divided into twelve heats and a final, Lord Nuffield entered the same three Hawker Tomtits, G-ABAX, G-AASI and G-ABOD, that had taken part in the 1933 Air Race, but flown on this occasion by Wg-Cdr J.W. Woodhouse DSO, MC, W.H. Sutcliffe and George Lowdell respectively. While G-ABAX and G-AASI were fitted with Wolseley A.R.9 Mark IA engines, G-ABOD had an A.R.9 Mark IIA engine installed. (A list of the forty-one entrants in the 1934 King's Cup Air Race appears in Appendix 7.)

Although Sutcliffe and Lowdell were placed first and second respectively in heat one, Wg-Cdr Woodhouse would have achieved third place had his Tomtit not suffered a problem that could have had very serious consequences. Near to a turning point, when the Tomtit was about 60ft from the ground, the port aileron operating rod came adrift as a ball-headed bolt had become loose. This left only the starboard aileron operating but, being an experienced First World War pilot, Wg-Cdr Woodhouse managed to maintain control of the Tomtit and with careful rudder work he returned safely to the starting point of the race at Hatfield.

Sutcliffe, who was the Midland Aeroplane Club's instructor, won heat seven, during which Lowdell made a forced landing after his Tomtit's engine suffered fuel starvation due to a blocked vent pipe, thereby putting him out of the race. However, a few weeks later, George Lowdell had better luck when he piloted the same Tomtit (G-ABOD) in the Newcastle Trophy Race, from London to Newcastle, winning the second prize.

Hawker Tomtit G–ABOD, fitted with a Wolseley A.R.9., Aries Mk II engine.

Of the three Tomtits entered by Lord Nuffield in the 1934 King's Cup Air Race, only Sutcliffe's G–AASI[10] performed without incident and, having gained second position in the first heat of the semi-final (heat eleven), this aircraft was placed seventh in the final. According to *The Aeroplane*, 'Sutcliffe flew beautifully right up to the finish, but the handicap beat him' and they declared that, 'all three Wolseley motors ran perfectly'.[11]

Three weeks after the Air Race, *The Aeroplane* said an opportunity to visit Wolseley's factory, in Birmingham, was '… eagerly taken as being likely to give an insight into the ideas that are guiding Mr. W. Cannell, Managing Director of the company, in the present developments'. The magazine reported:

> Wolseley air-cooled aero-motors, the 185 hp A.R.9. and 145 hp A.R.7., are now in production. And the first Airspeed Envoy which is the first aeroplane with Wolseley motors as standard has already created a most favourable impression. Cheap in first costs, simple to maintain, and with Lord Nuffield's vast interests, as manifest in the Morris Motors Organization, to make easy the supply of spares all over the World. The fact that motors of such a nature are now available to builders of aeroplanes seems likely to play an important part in the extension of commercial aviation, - particularly because the cost of the motors is such a large proportion of the cost of the complete aeroplane.[12]

Wolseley encouraged feedback by asking operators of their aero engines to make suggestions, 'for improvements in the engine, its equipment, accessibility or servicing…' The company also promoted their ability to, 'provide efficient and dependable service wherever their engines are stationed and operated' and stated, '…spares will always be available at reasonable charges'. To foster goodwill, users of Wolseley aero engines were 'cordially invited' to visit the works in order 'to inspect engines in their various stages of production and to discuss any problems on installation or servicing matters or such that may arise'. Wolseley said that their aero engines were made in 'an engineering factory which is one of the most up-to-date and finest equipped in Europe' and that they had 'been subjected to, and had successfully passed, the Air Ministry type test'.[13]

By 1936 Wolseley had introduced the following range of air-cooled radial aero engines, which were all named after the signs of the Zodiac.

Three views of Wolseley's aero engine factory at Ward End, Birmingham, in 1934.

Top: The aero engine inspection department.

Middle: The machine shops.

Bottom: A Wolseley A.R.9. Aries, running on test with a wind brake. Note the observer in a sheltered office.

Above and left: The
Wolseley A.R.7., Aquarius.

WOLSELEY RADIAL AERO ENGINES AVAILABLE IN 1936

1) A.R.7. Aquarius

Described by Wolseley Aero Engines Ltd as 'Ideal for Ab Initio Training. Robust and Economical. Built for hard work'.

Right: The induction fan for the Wolseley A.R.7. Aquarius. A similar induction fan is fitted to the Wolseley A.R.9. Aries, Mk III, and the Wolseley Scorpio.

Below: A cut-away view of the Wolseley A.R.7. Aquarius. (*Aeroplane/*www.aeroplanemonthly.com)

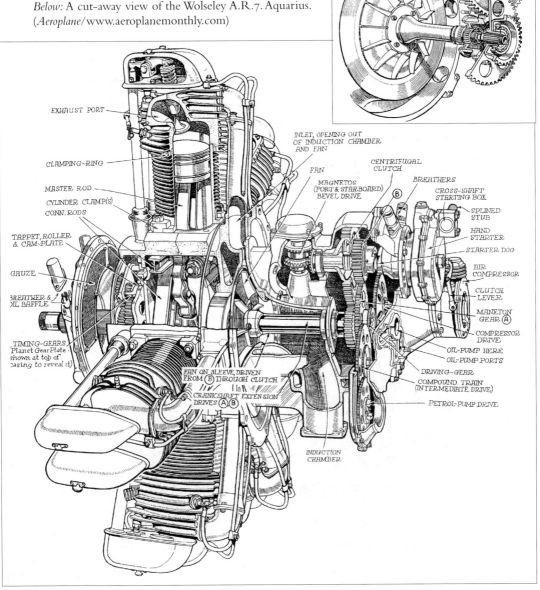

General Specification

Type	Air-cooled Radial
Number of cylinders	7
Bore	4³/₁₆in
Stroke	4¾in
Capacity	458 cu. in
Capacity	7.5 litres
Compression ratio	5.3 : 1
Carburetter and type	S.U.A.V.18
Induction fan ratio	3.8 times engine speed
Magnetos and type	Twin B.T.H. S.C.7.
Tappets	Manually adjusted
Airscrew reduction	nil (direct drive)
Direction of rotation	R.H. Tractor
Dry weight (including airscrew hub and hand starter)	320lb
Overall diameter	40¼in

Provision is made for the fitment of an air compressor, twin fuel pumps and an electric starter.

Performance

Normal bhp	155
Normal rpm	2,250
Maximum bhp	168
Maximum rpm	2,475
Petrol consumption at 75 per cent of max. power	0.53pts/bhp/hr
Oil consumption	1.5–3pts/hr
Specific weight	1.90lb/bhp

Note

(1) The normal bhp for A.R.7, Aquarius was initially quoted as 145.

(2) The A.R.7, Aquarius follows the general lines of the A.R.9, Aries except that the A.R.7 has seven cylinders and the A.R.9 has nine.

2) A.R.9 Aries

Described by Wolseley Aero Engines Ltd as being for 'Advanced Training and Communication Aircraft. Economical to operate, easily maintained. Fitted with every modern equipment'.

General specification

	Mark I 185hp	Mark II 185hp	Mark III 205hp
Type	Air-cooled radial	Air-cooled radial	Air-cooled radial
Number of cylinders	9	9	9
Bore	4³/₁₆in	4³/₁₆in	4³/₁₆in
Stroke	4¾in	4¾in	4¾in
Capacity	588.6 cu. in	588.6 cu. in	588.6 cu. in
Capacity	9.65 litres	9.65 litres	9.65 litres
Compression ratio	5.3 : 1	5.3 : 1	5.4 : 1

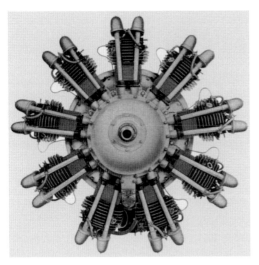

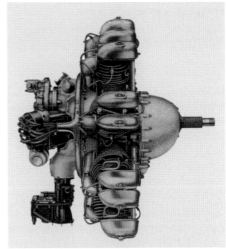

This page: The Wolseley A.R.9. Aries, Mark I.

	Mark I 185hp	Mark II 185hp	Mark III 205hp
Carburetter, make and type	Claudel Hobson A.V.64B	Claudel Hobson A.V.64B	S.U.A.V.20
Induction fan ratio	–	–	3.8 times engine speed
Magnetos, make and type	Twin B.T.H. S.C.9	Twin B.T.H. S.C.9	Twin B.T.H. S.C.9
Tappets	Manually adjusted	Manually adjusted	Manually adjusted
Airscrew reduction type	Internal spur gear	nil (direct drive)	Epicyclic
Airscrew reduction ratio	0.621: 1	–	0.629: 1
Direction of rotation	R.H. Tractor	R.H. Tractor	R.H. Tractor
Dry weight, including airscrew hub and hand starter	452lb	372lb	510lb
Overall diameter	41¼in	41¼in	41¼in
Overall length	38¼in	31⅞in	42in
Length – mounting plate to back of airscrew	18⅞in	13⁹/₁₆in	18.16in

Performance

	Mark I 185hp	Mark II 185hp	Mark III 205hp
Normal bhp	185	185	205
Normal rpm	2,200	2,200	2,250
Maximum bhp	203	203	225
Maximum rpm	2,420	2,420	2,475
Petrol consumption at 90 per cent power	0.562 pts/bhp/hr	0.562 pts/bhp/hr	0.545 pts/bhp/hr
Oil consumption	3½pts/hr	2½pts/hr	3½pts/hr
Specific weight	2.23lb/bhp	1.83lb/bhp	2.26lb/bhp

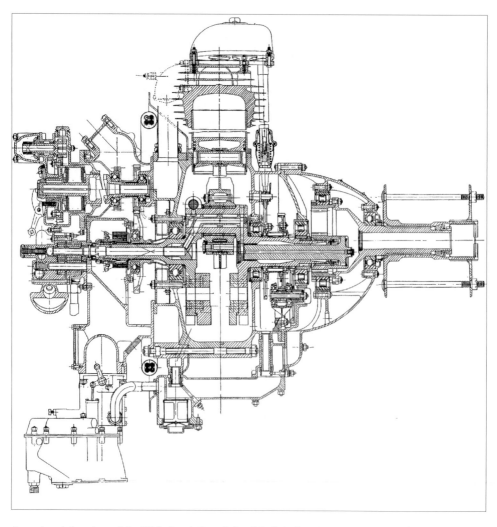

A sectional drawing of the Wolseley A.R.9. Aries, Mark I, showing its airscrew reduction gear of internal spur gear type; note that the airscrew shaft is offset to the centre line of the crankshaft. (*Aeroplane*/www.aeroplanemonthly.com)

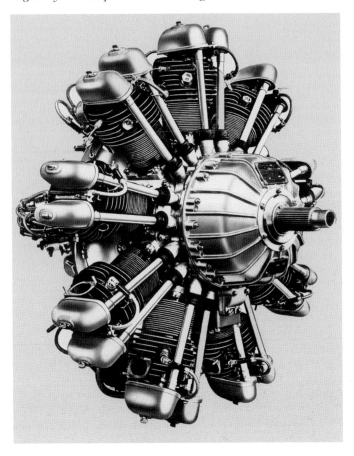

Above and right: The
Wolseley A.R.9. Aries,
Mark III, with an airscrew
reduction gear of epicyclic
type.

Notes

(1) Provision is made for the fitment of a generator, twin fuel pumps, electric starter, air compressor and vacuum pump
(2) Many parts of the A.R.9., Aries are interchangeable with the A.R.7, Aquarius.

3) Scorpio

Described by Wolseley Aero Engines Ltd as being 'For the small fast multi-engined aircraft'.

General specification

	Mark I. 230hp	*Mark II. 250hp*
Type	Air-cooled radial	Air-cooled radial
Number of cylinders	9	9
Bore	4³/₈in	4³/₈in
Stroke	4¾in	4¾in
Capacity	643 cu. in	643 cu. in
Capacity	10.53 litres	10.53 litres
Compression ratio	5.4:1	6.5:1
		(87 Octane)
Carburetter, make and type	S.U. A.V.20	S.U. A.V.20
Induction fan ratio	3.8 times engine speed	7.3 times engine speed
Magnetos, make and type	Twin B.T.H. SC9-5B	Twin B.T.H. SC9-5B
Tappets	Self adjusting hydraulic	Self adjusting hydraulic
Airscrew reduction type	Epicyclic	Epicyclic
Airscrew reduction	0.629:1	0.629:1
Direction of rotation	R.H. Tractor	R.H. Tractor
Dry weight, including airscrew hub and hand starter	536lb	550lb
Overall diameter	41¼in	41in
Overall length	42.15in	-
Length - mounting plate to back of airscrew	18¼in	-

Performance

	Mark I. 230hp	*Mark II. 250hp*
Normal bhp	230	250
Normal rpm	2,250	2,250
Maximum bhp	250	290 at 6,700ft
Maximum rpm	2,475	2,600
Rated altitude	-	5,000ft
bhp at sea level, rated boost normal rpm	-	244
bhp at sea level, mpb for take off, normal rpm	-	270
Fuel consumption at 75% power	0.53 pts/bhp/hr	-

Fuel consumption, rated boost, normal rpm		0.6 pts/hr
Fuel consumption, cruising at rated altitude, normal rpm	–	0.5pts/bhp/hr
Oil consumption	3 to 4.5pts/hr	–
Specific weight	2.14lb/bhp	1.89lb/bhp

Notes

(1) The normal bhp for the Scorpio Mark I was initially quoted as 225.

(2) Scorpio Mark I. Provision is made for an air compressor, twin fuel pumps and an electric starter.

(3) Scorpio Mark II. Provision is made for a generator, twin fuel pumps, air compressor, electric starter, fluid pump, vacuum pump and spare drive.

(4) The Scorpio, which passed its type test in July 1935, shares a common length of stroke with the A.R.7., Aquarius and the A.R.9., Aries. Unlike the A.R.7. and the A.R.9., the Scorpio has self-adjusting tappets.

(5) At first, the Scorpio was called the Taurus. The name was changed when Wolseley found that the Taurus had already been registered by the Bristol Aeroplane Co. Ltd.

Above and right: The Wolseley Scorpio Mark I.

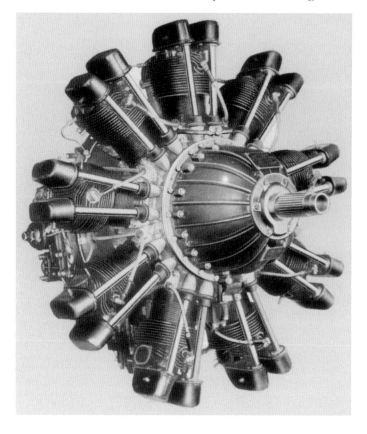

Above and left: The
Wolseley Scorpio
Mark II.

4) Libra

Described by Wolseley Aero Engines Ltd as being 'In the vanguard of Modern Aircraft requirements'.

General Specification

Type	Air-cooled Radial
Number of cylinders	9
Bore	5in
Stroke	5.5in
Capacity	970 cu. in
Capacity	15.9 litres
Compression ratio	6.5 to 1 (87 octane)
Tappets	Self-adjusting hydraulic
Airscrew reduction	0.606 to 1
Direction of rotation	R.H. Tractor
Dry weight	725lb
Overall diameter	44½in
Length, mounting plate to rear of airscrew	23⁵/₈in
Length, mounting plate to extreme rear	20½in

Performance

Rated altitude	6,000ft
bhp at rated altitude, normal rpm, full throttle	440
Normal rpm	2,400
Maximum bhp	505 at 7300ft
Maximum rpm	2,750
bhp at sea level, rated boost, normal rpm	412
bhp at sea level, mpb for take off, normal rpm	495
Fuel consumption, rated boost at sea level	0.6pts/bhp/hr
Fuel consumption, cruising at normal rpm and rated altitude	0.5 pts/bhp/hr
Specific weight	1.43lb/bhp

Explanation of abbreviations

bhp:	brake horse power
cu. in:	cubic inches
ft:	feet
in:	inches
lb:	pounds
lbs/bhp:	pounds per brake horse power
mpb:	maximum permissible boost
pts/bhp/hr :	pints per brake horse power per hour
pts/hr:	pints per hour
RH:	Right Hand
rpm:	revolutions per minute

Above and left: The
Wolseley Libra.

Above and left: This engine, which appears to be a development of the Wolseley A.R.9. Aries, Mark III, is most probably a Wolseley Leo.

WOLSELEY RADIAL AERO ENGINES UNDER DEVELOPMENT, 1935/1936

1) The Leo: development of this aero engine, which produced 280hp at 6,000ft, ceased in 1936.

2) The Gemini: this compact, eighteen-cylinder, double-row radial aero engine, super-charged to 565hp at 6,000ft, was undergoing flight development tests, before its final type test and being placed into production, at the time Wolseley Aero Engines Ltd was closed down in August 1936.

A technical specification for these engines does not appear to have been issued.

GENERAL DESCRIPTION OF THE WOLSELEY SCORPIO, MK I, RADIAL AERO ENGINE

The nine-cylinder 230hp Wolseley Scorpio radial aero engine is based on the seven-cylinder Wolseley Aquarius A.R.7, but has larger diameter cylinder bores, self-adjusting hydraulically operated tappets, an airscrew reduction gear and other detail differences.

Crankcase

The crankcase is made in two halves produced from heat-treated duralmin castings and split transversely along the centre line of the cylinders. When bolted together the two halves, which have well-ribbed internal diaphragms, form a stiff and rigid foundation of the engine. Stamped steel housings which are shrunk and bolted into the crankcase diaphragms, carry the two main bearings for the crank-shaft. The timing gear chamber, formed by the front half of the crankcase, contains the cam gear and hydraulic tappet mechanisms. This chamber is enclosed by a coni-cal cover that carries a roller bearing to support the front end of the crankshaft. The diaphragm in this half is fitted with pivots to locate the tappet rockers while a plate, perma-nently secured to the rear half of the crankcase, forms one side of the induction chamber; the other side of this chamber is formed by the induction fan shroud. An induction ring is attached to the rear edge of the crankcase and a circular pressed-steel mounting plate, to enable the engine to be connected to the air-frame, is sandwiched between this ring and the crankcase.

Crankshaft

The single throw, two-piece, drop-forged crankshaft is machined all over and made of nickel-chrome molybdenum steel. Two balance weights are each secured to the crank-shaft by a pair of high-tensile steel bolts, in addition to a turned register. The maneton is attached to the crankpin by a key and a clamped eye, the pinch bolt for which has a definite length so that when tightening the nut, the stress in the bolt can be limited by measuring its extension. The crankshaft assembly runs in three bearings; two rollers at the front and one ball at the rear, the latter also provides end-wise location. The crankshaft and the crank pin are drilled for lightness. These drillings are fitted with removable duralumin plugs, to provide a continuous oilway of uniform section thereby preventing a build-up of sludge when using mineral lubricating oil. To ensure smooth running, the crankshaft assembly is dynamically balanced.

This advertisement appeared in July 1936.

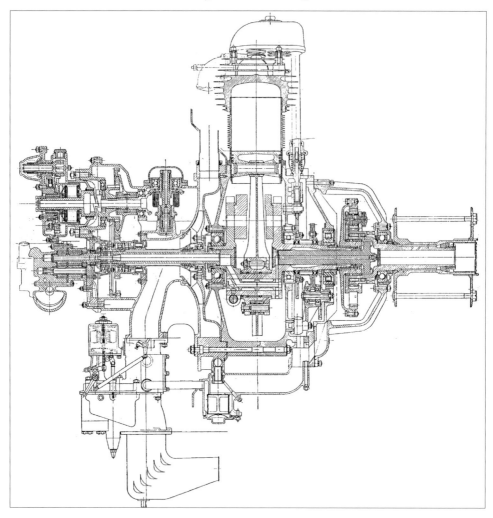

A sectional drawing of the Wolseley Scorpio, showing its S.U. A.V.20 Carburetter, induction fan and epicyclic type of reduction gear.

The Master Connecting Rod

The master connecting rod is located in No.1 (top) cylinder and is made from nickel-chrome molybdenum steel. The shank of the rod is of 'H' section and is machined all over. Its solid big-end has a floating steel bush, white-metalled inside and out, that is provided with numerous oil holes to ensure adequate lubrication.

The Auxiliary Connecting Rods

The auxiliary connecting rods are also made of nickel-chrome molybdenum steel and are of 'H' section. Hard phosphor bronze bushes are driven into both ends of each connecting rod and special provision is made so that if these bushes turn, a supply of oil will be maintained. The auxiliary rods are attached to the big-end of the master rod by hardened steel wrist pins that are retained by set screws. When tightened, these set screws draw the

The crankshaft assembly.

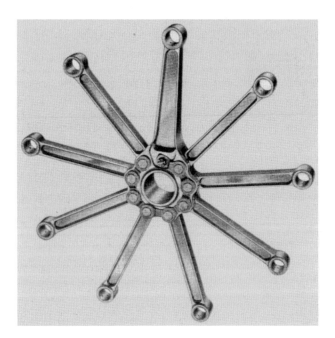

The connecting rod assembly, showing the master connecting rod and eight auxiliary connecting rods.

tapered ends of the wrist pins into correspondingly formed holes in one web of the big-end. The set screws are secured by lock plates and each wrist pin is provided with a key to prevent the pin from rotating.

Cylinders

The cylinders are of composite type, machined all over and having close-pitched shallow fins; each cylinder has a capacity of 1,170cc, giving a total capacity for the engine of 10,530cc. The barrels are made from carbon steel forgings and they are shrunk and screwed to cast aluminium alloy cylinder heads. To reinforce the joints between the barrels and the cylinder heads, steel bands, each with a pair of fins, are pressed onto the lower end of the cylinder heads to prevent any leakage of pressure at working temperatures. The valve seats, which are made of monal metal to withstand corrosion in case fuel containing tetraethyl lead is used, are screwed and shrunk into the dome-shaped combustion chambers.

A cylinder assembly.

A deep spigot and a flange are provided at the lower ends of the cylinder assemblies. Each assembly is secured to the crankcase by four steel clamps that are held by headed studs and nuts. The studs are screwed and locked into position from the inside of the crankcase, so that most of the tension load is taken by their heads rather than by their threads.

Pistons

The fully skirted pistons are machined all over and are made from drop forged heat-treated aluminium alloy. Two pressure and two scraper rings are fitted to each piston, one of the latter being an oil control type, and the fully floating gudgeon pins are retained by circlips.

The Valve Gear

Each cylinder is fitted with a single exhaust and a single inlet valve, which are inclined and interchangeable. The valves, each of which is fitted with double valve springs, are located in renewable phosphor bronze guides. They are made of nickel chrome steel, with hardened steel buttons on their stems, and are operated by rockers that are mounted on needle roller bearings. These bearings are located in brackets which are secured to the cylinder head in such a way to prevent loosening under working conditions. Steel rollers are positioned on the ends of the rockers that abut the valve stems, and each cylinder is fitted with two detachable pressed-aluminium covers to enclose the rocker gear.

The roller-ended tappet rockers, oscillated by the cam that is driven by a double train of hardened spur-gears, lift the hydraulic, self-adjusting, tappets. The inner and outer members of the telescopic tappets are positioned in bosses which are contained in a ring that is secured to the front diaphragm of the crankcase. This ring has an annular oil passage

Views of pistons.

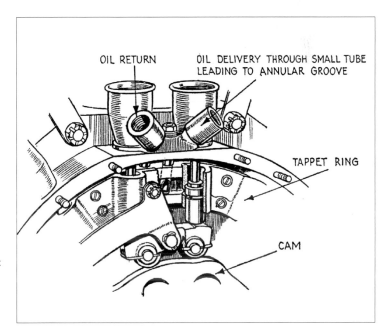

The hydraulic tappet arrangement, the operation of which is explained in the text.

from which drillings align with a groove around each tappet, when the tappet is at its innermost position. Oil passes under pressure into these grooves and through ports in the outer member of a tappet. The oil then displaces the inner member of the tappet until all the tappet clearance is taken up. As soon as the inner tappet begins to lift, the oil supply is cut off and a pad of oil is then trapped between the two tappet members. The inner tappet then operates another tappet, located in a long bronze guide that is secured to the crankcase, which in turn actuates the valve rocker via a push rod. The tubular steel push rods have hardened steel cups fitted to each end; they are enclosed in aluminium tubes and an oil seal is provided at their crankcase end by cups covered with oil-resisting rubber sleeves.

When the hydraulic tappet moves back to its innermost position, the drillings from the annular passage once again align with the groove in the tappet. Since the tappet clearance varies during the running of the engine, due to temperature variations, the quantity of oil trapped between the inner and outer members of the tappet alters according to requirements, hence providing a self-adjustment. Should any oil be squeezed from the tappets during their operation, the leakage is confined to the interior of the engine.

This hydraulic tappet arrangement, which not only provides a neat and compact construction but also reduces the need for external oil supply pipes, is covered by Wolseley's patent No.422,408.

Induction System

A 2⅛in diameter, type A.V.20, S.U. carburetter, fitted with an adjustable tapered needle positioned inside a jet, supplies the air/fuel mixture. Movement of the throttle lever alters the position of the needle which varies the fuel flow from the jet to suit the throttle setting. Alternative needles can be fitted, with each size giving a difference in petrol flow of about three pints per hour. A corrugated pressure capsule, similar to that used in an aneroid barometer, automatically repositions the needle and thereby adjusts the fuel flow to suit the altitude of the aircraft. In addition, an air passage transfers the air intake pressure to the float chamber of the carburetter, so that the amount of fuel flowing from the float chamber is varied in accordance with the air intake pressure. For improving the acceleration of the engine, an accelerator pump, operated by the throttle lever, is fitted.

The engine is provided with a dynamically balanced induction fan that is machined all over to achieve a minimum of clearance between the fan blades and the sides of the fan chamber. A series of gears, one of which contains a centrifugal clutch that slips under sudden changes in load, enables the induction fan to revolve at 3.8 times engine speed. The fan is driven via a spring, to prevent shocks being transmitted to it when rapid fluctuations in engine speed occur. The rearward projection of the fan shroud forms a sleeve, concentric with the fan's drive shaft, which then sweeps down to a flange for mounting the carburetter.

The air/fuel mixture from the carburetter is fed by the fan to an annular induction chamber that is heated by scavenged oil, contained in a jacket round the chamber. This arrangement of transferring the oil's heat to the air/fuel mixture, through the common wall separating the induction chamber and the oil jacket, also has the benefit of cooling the engine oil; it is covered by Wolseley's patent No.348,471. From the induction chamber, the air/fuel mixture is fed via an induction ring to each cylinder by radial aluminium pipes that are attached to the inlet ports by cast elbows.

Although the induction fan should not be regarded as a supercharger, as its purpose is to mix the air/fuel mixture to obtain a good distribution, it does provide a slight positive pressure in the induction chamber.

Ignition

The ignition system is duplicated. Two sparking plugs are fitted to each cylinder, in bronze adaptors, and a pair of B.T.H., type S.C.9, magnetos are driven by bevel gears off a central vertical shaft. A patented (No.347,552) form of spring drive is fitted to relieve both magnetos of the crankshaft's torsional vibrations; a simple method of adjusting the tension of the spring is provided. The outer end of clock-type spring is attached to a sleeve, secured to the drive shaft, while the other end engages with the driving bevel. The amount of angular movement in the magneto drive is limited by a key positioned in a slot.

All of the high-tension ignition cables are enclosed in an aluminium conduit that is mounted at the rear of the engine.

Published in July 1934, this is probably the first advertisement issued by Wolseley to promote their radial aero engines. The A.R.9. and A.R.7. engines were later given the names Aries and Aquarius respectively.

Airscrew Reduction Gear

The airscrew reduction gear is of epicyclic type giving a ratio of 0.629:1; this provides an airscrew speed of 1,415rpm at a normal engine speed of 2,250rpm. The sun gear, airscrew shaft and satellite pinions form a complete assembly which can be detached from the engine, for inspection, in a few minutes. The airscrew hub is made from a steel forging and is attached to the airscrew shaft by splines, with bronze cones at either end of the hub. A nut, which secures the airscrew shaft to the hub, is locked by a special cup held by a heavy rectangular section circlip.

Lubrication

A dry sump system is employed with scavenge and pressure pumps, contained in one unit, driven at crankshaft speed off the tailshaft via a universal coupling. Both pumps are spur gear type; the driving gears are made of steel and the driven gears in phosphor bronze. The pressure pump delivers 140 gallons of oil per hour, at 2,200rpm, while the scavenge pump has double this capacity. The oil filter chamber is integral with the casing of the oil pumps and a relief valve opens if its fabric filter, which is supported by a heavy gauge wire framework of star section, becomes blocked. The filter element should be removed for cleaning at intervals of approximately 100 hours running time.

Oil is delivered to the engine, at a pressure of 40 to 60lb per sq. in, through the driving spindle of the pump to the hollow shaft of the maneton. This oil then passes through the drilled passages in the maneton web to the crankpin where much of it lubricates the big-end bearing, the leakage from which splash lubricates the pistons and cylinder walls. The rest of the oil passes through the forward end of the crankshaft and into the interior of the airscrew reduction gear assembly by way of a restricted feed and the hollow torque shaft. The oil then issues from a jet and enters the chamber formed at the inner end of the airscrew shaft, thereby lubricating its rear bearing. Grooves and drillings lead the oil to the centres of each satellite gear spindle so that the floating bushes of the satellite gears receive adequate lubrication. This method of supplying oil to the airscrew reduction gear is detailed in Wolseley's patent No.352,753.

The auxiliary drives are lubricated by a bleed from the oil jacket positioned round the induction chamber. This bleed feeds oil to the socket for the lower end of the vertical magneto shaft and a spiral groove, cut into the phosphor bronze bush fitted to this socket, draws oil into the rear casing for the lubrication of the gears and bearings in the casing. Oil is also fed up the centre of the vertical shaft to lubricate the spring-driven sleeve of the magneto drive bevel.

Drainage ducts are provided to enable the oil to flow into the sump, which is located between the bottom pair of cylinders, from where it passes to the scavenge pump via the oil jacket positioned round the induction chamber and a wire gauze strainer; a thermometer connection is provided in the oil return pipe.

Great care has been taken to prevent oil leakage. All joint faces are of large area and they are secured by an adequate number of bolts and studs.

Starting System

A circular flange is provided at the rear of the engine for the attachment of the Wolseley patented (No.352,735) hand-turning gear, which is fitted as standard. This hand-turning gear has a ratio of 8:1 and it incorporates a ratchet device so that, in the event of the engine turning in the reverse direction due to a backfire, the plates of the driving clutch will slip thereby preventing injury to the operator. An Eclipse inertia starter or a Rotax type Y.150 electric starter could be supplied as alternatives.

A priming system, having connections to a spray nozzle in each cylinder head, can be used to assist cold starting.

The Wolseley hand-turning gear.

Auxiliaries and Optional Extras

Mountings are provided on the rear cover of the engine for the fitment of an Amal duplex diaphragm petrol pump, a BTH air compressor and a Rotax 500 watt generator. A right-angled skew gear is fitted to the oil pump for driving a rev. counter at one-quarter engine speed.

A Townend ring could be supplied, as could an aluminised exhaust collector ring.

Finish

To prevent corrosion, and to maintain a good finish, all exposed parts of the engine are plated with cadmium and, in addition, the barrels and cylinder heads are finished with special heat-resisting enamel.

Notes

1   *Flight*, 4 June 1925, p.335v.
2   Adeney, Martin, p.141.
3   Bulman, George Purvis, p.244.
4   Bulman, George Purvis, p.244.
5   *Flight*, 13 July 1933, p.688.
6   *Flight*, 13 July 1933, p.699.
7   Sqd. Ldr George H. Reid retired from the RAF in 1927 and then formed Reid Manufacturing & Construction Co. Ltd to manufacture aircraft instruments of his own invention. In 1928, Frederick Sigrist, Hawker's joint managing director, loaned his name to Reid's activities and the pair formed Reid & Sigrist Ltd. As well as making aircraft instruments, this company later built a twin-engine trainer aircraft.
8   Leasor, James, p.134.
9   Leasor, James, p.135.
10 G-AASI was disposed of by Wolseley Motors Ltd, to J.G. Hopcraft in February 1936 and, flown by Flt Off. C.F. Hughesdon, was entered in the Manx Air Races of June that year. At an average speed of 107mph, 'ASI came in a very good second in the race from London to the island, but only managed tenth position in the Manx Air Derby. In September 1936, Wolseley put Hawker Tomtits G-ABOD and G-ABAX up for sale, the S.U. Carburetter Co. taking them on temporary charge. See Mason, Francis, K., p.156.
11 *The Aeroplane*, 18 July 1934, p.81.
12 *The Aeroplane*, 8 August 1934, p.173.
13 Instruction handbook for the Wolseley Scorpio, Mark I; September 1935.

3

WOLSELEY AERO ENGINES LTD AND CONCERNS ABOUT SUPER TAX

In October 1932 Lord Nuffield celebrated his fifty-fifth birthday. He was immensely wealthy, but both he and his advisors were becoming increasingly worried by the possible effect of Estate Duties on his personally owned companies because, at that time, the Duties on large estates were 40 per cent. Immense wealth can also bring other problems which, in the case of Lord Nuffield, included claims by the Inland Revenue for Super Tax. The Inland Revenue claimed that Lord Nuffield, as dominant shareholder, had used his position to hold back most of the profits in his companies in order to avoid the imposition of Super Tax which would have been due if the profits had been distributed and become part of his income.

Super Tax, which was paid in addition to ordinary Income Tax, was levied against individuals whose annual income was more than £2,000 per annum (about £90,000 at 2006 values). Unlike Income Tax, which was levied at fixed rates, Super Tax increased progressively with rising income and, as a company only paid income tax at the standard rate, there were advantages in leaving money in a company.

Two directions for assessment of Super Tax were made by the Inland Revenue in the case of Morris Motors Ltd, for financial years 1922/23 and 1927/28, and the appeals against them were heard in the High Court during November 1926 and December 1929. Both appeals were won by Morris Motors which was able to show that any profits that had not been distributed had been used for the maintenance and development of its business.

The first assessment made Lord Nuffield more conscious of the need for a sound tax-efficient corporate structure and so, in June 1926, Morris Motors Ltd became a public company when £3 million in Cumulative Preference Shares were issued for cash and Morris Motors (1926) Ltd was formed. At the same time this company absorbed Osberton Radiators Ltd, Morris Engines Ltd, (previously Hotchkiss et Cie.) and Hollick & Pratt Ltd, until then all separately owned by Lord Nuffield, and these companies then became known as Morris Motors Ltd – Radiators Branch, Engines Branch and Bodies Branch respectively. Also, on 27 July 1927, a holding company was registered, Morris Industries Ltd, to enable Lord Nuffield to move funds between his companies without incurring tax liabilities and to acquire the S.U. Co. Ltd.

The sale of Preference Shares generated great wealth for Lord Nuffield which he used not only to develop his business but also to start his activities as a generous benefactor. Furthermore, as all of the Ordinary Shares in Morris Motors (1926) Ltd[1] were retained by Lord Nuffield, he remained in a position whereby 'he could control the company as if he were the sole proprietor'.[2]

Lord Nuffield.

After the second Super Tax assessment [at the end of 1929] Lord Nuffield became convinced that, by a change in the law or for other reasons, it would eventually be impossible to continue his vigorous policy of keeping back profits if the equity continued to be his personal property. If these profits were then to become liable to Super Tax, Morris Motors' reserves might suffer a very heavy and sudden depletion. At the same time, the main line of his business was well established and it would not, he thought, be long before a more usual type of organisation might be suitable. He therefore decided he should think about putting his shares on the market - and would probably have done this soon had the depression not come.[3]

Following the Great Depression of the early 1930s, the general recovery in trade by 1935 brought better stock market conditions which made it feasible for Lord Nuffield to merge some of his remaining personally owned companies with Morris Motors Ltd, and to offer some of his Ordinary Shares in that company on the London Stock Exchange. Although permission to deal had been obtained for the whole of the £2,650,000 Ordinary stock, it was decided to place only a quarter of the whole (2,650,000 5s units) Lord Nuffield retaining the rest himself.[4] The shares were made available to the market, during October 1936, at 37s 6d and dealings started at 39s. Public demand was so strong that after a hectic first day's trading, the shares closed at 41s 10½d (£2.09) which generated even more wealth for Lord Nuffield, who then increased the number of his benefactions and formed trusts as well as endowments and schemes to benefit his employees.

   These actions were considered the best way of minimising both Estate Duties and Super Tax liabilities. In addition, they were welcomed by Lord Nuffield's financial and legal advisors as they had been concerned that Preference Shareholders of Morris Motors Ltd might take exception to Lord Nuffield, as chairman, buying components for that business from companies which were in his personal ownership. Accordingly, Wolseley Motors (1927) Ltd[5]

This advertisement for the Wolseley A.R.7. Aquarius, issued in the name of Wolseley Motors (1927) Ltd, appeared in June 1935, shortly before Wolseley Aero Engines Ltd was formed.

W.M.W. (Miles) Thomas, left, and Lord Nuffield.

and the M.G. Car Co. Ltd were sold to Morris Motors Ltd on 1 July 1935. Fifteen months later, in October 1936, Morris Motors Ltd bought Morris Commercial Cars Ltd, the S.U. Carburetter Co. Ltd and Morris Industries Exports Ltd.

While Lord Nuffield was prepared to finance the development and manufacture of Wolseley aero engines himself, he did not consider that people who bought Ordinary Shares in Morris Motors Ltd should bear the risks of the aero engine project. And so, three days before Wolseley Motors (1927) Ltd was sold to Morris Motors Ltd, Wolseley Aero Engines Ltd[6] was formed, on 27 June 1935, to take over Wolseley's aero engine business, with Lord Nuffield as governing director and William Cannell as managing director. On his appointment, Cannell vacated a similar position with Wolseley Motors (1927) Ltd and this post was then filled by W.M.W. (Miles) Thomas DFC, who had been a fighter pilot during the First World War.[7]

When the mergers with Morris Motors Ltd had been completed, Wolseley Aero Engines Ltd and The Morris Garages Ltd became the only companies to remain in Lord Nuffield's personal ownership.

Although the costs of maintaining Wolseley's aero engine project, including the purchase of three Hawker Tomtits and two Airspeed Envoy aircraft for testing and demonstration purposes, from its beginnings in 1929 until the formation of Wolseley Aero Engines Ltd in June 1935, have not, so far, been found, they are estimated to be at least £350,000. These costs were presumably absorbed by Wolseley Motors (1927) Ltd, which was owned personally by Lord Nuffield as already mentioned. Fortunately, however, the financial accounts for Wolseley Aero Engines Ltd have survived and they show that in the fourteen months between 1 July 1935 until 31 August 1936, the company recorded a net loss of £59,363 4s 8d of which £39,284 6s 4d was a trading loss. Therefore, the costs involved in operating Wolseley's aero engine project between 1929 and 1936, are estimated to be over £410,000 (about £18.5 million at 2006 values).

The extent of Lord Nuffield's financial support for Wolseley Aero Engines Ltd, to keep the company afloat while it developed its business and endeavoured to find a market for its range of aero engines, is revealed in the ledgers of Morris Industries Ltd, the holding company for his personal investments. These ledgers show that on 12 July 1935, 10,000 Ordinary Shares in Wolseley Aero Engines Ltd were bought for £10,000, and that between July 1935 and July 1936, Morris Industries Ltd loaned Wolseley Aero Engines Ltd £165,500, giving a total investment, in a little over twelve months, of £175,500 (about £8 million at 2006 values).

Notes

1   The (1926) was dropped from the company's name in August 1929.

2   Andrews & Brunner, p.162.

3   Andrews & Brunner, p174.

4   Andrews and Brunner, p.212.

5   On being sold to Morris Motors Ltd, the '1927' was dropped from the company's name.

6   The directors' minutes of Wolseley Aero Engines Ltd note that the company bought the business of aircraft engine manufacture carried on by Wolseley Motors (1927) Ltd at their factory in Drews Lane, Ward End, Birmingham, and all the assets of such business (including plant, machinery, tools, stock in trade, patents, designs and effects as used by Wolseley Motors (1927) Ltd for the manufacture and development of aircraft engines) for the sum of £50,957 17s 10d.

7   Miles Thomas became the managing director of Morris Motors Ltd and Lord Nuffield's deputy in 1940 and was appointed chairman of the British Overseas Airways Corporation in 1949. He was knighted in 1943 and became a life peer, Lord Thomas of Remenham, in 1971.

4

THE MARKET FOR WOLSELEY AERO ENGINES

A) THE PRIVATE MARKET

The rapid growth in the number of privately owned aircraft registered between 1927 and 1930 was not sustained during the early 1930s, owing to the Great Depression which followed the Wall Street Crash of 29 October 1929. Between 1930 and 1933, the year that Wolseley aero engines were first exhibited in public, the number of privately owned aircraft held on the Air Ministry's Register increased by only seventy-five. To make matters worse, the rise in the number of pilots who qualified annually with a class 'A' licence at the Government sponsored Light Aeroplane Clubs, which had been evident during the late 1920s, was reversed in the early 1930s.

The opportunity to sell aero engines in quantity for privately owned aircraft, which Lord Nuffield had anticipated in 1929, had not, therefore, materialised, so, apart from Airspeed Ltd (a company which will be discussed later), Wolseley found it very difficult to find a market for its aero engines among airframe manufacturers.

It was, perhaps, no coincidence that the widely circulated *Morris Owner* magazine, published by a subsidiary company of Morris Motors Ltd, carried an article in its September 1933 edition entitled 'Flying as a Motorist Sees it'. The author, Lord Cardigan, compared private flying with driving a motor car and declared, 'No one, having once learned to enjoy the power of swift travel over ground, can well fail to comprehend the pleasure of a swifter travel through the unrestricted spaces of the air'.

A few months later, the *Morris Owner* published another, but more comprehensive, article, headed 'Flying for the Car Owner' which encouraged people to learn to fly and to purchase a light aircraft. After giving details of some of the more popular light aircraft which were available, ranging in price from £595 to over £1,000, the article promoted the Light Aeroplane Clubs where, 'for a sum of £20 or so any ordinarily healthy person should be able to obtain his 'A' licence, as instruction is given on the school machines at a cost of £2 to £2 10s per hour'. It continued:

> All that has to be accomplished to qualify for this licence is three hours solo flying, and two very simple tests. One of these is a height test which consists of climbing to 2,000 feet, closing the throttle, gliding down and landing within 50 yards of a pre-arranged mark. The other is a series of right and left-hand turns made around two points on the ground, and then landing as in the first test. The rules of the air must also be mastered, but these, being simpler than the rules of the road, present no difficulty whatever. After qualification, machines can be hired for as low as 30s per hour for solo flying.

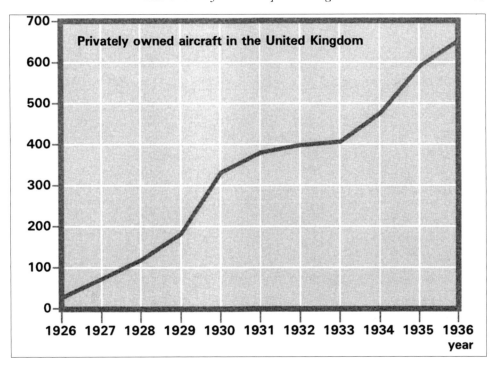

'To help the potential owner-pilot who is still hesitating to come to a decision', the costs of maintaining a light aircraft, for an average yearly mileage of 12,000, were detailed as follows:

	£	s	d
Petrol and oil	40	16	8
Certificate of Airworthiness	5	5	0
Tyres (subject to modification)	3	12	6
Engine and aircraft overhaul	70	0	0
Housing (private lock-up garage)	39	0	0
	£158	14	2 or 3*d* per mile

The article concluded by saying that:

> flying is one of the most fascinating hobbies one can adopt; it has been proved by statistics to be as safe as, if not safer than, any other mode of transport, and the combination of an aeroplane and a car is as near the ideal as it is possible to get.[1]

B) THE GOVERNMENT MARKET

In an effort to find another market with more potential, Wolseley's managing director, William Cannell, made contact with the Air Ministry but, in reply to a letter sent during November 1933 promoting two types of their aero engines, Cannell was told, 'As explained verbally, I think it improbable that the Air Ministry will be in a position to utilise either of the types of engine you describe in your letter'.[2]

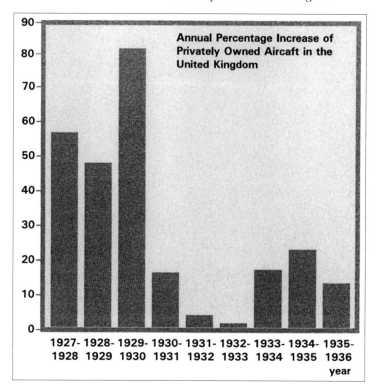

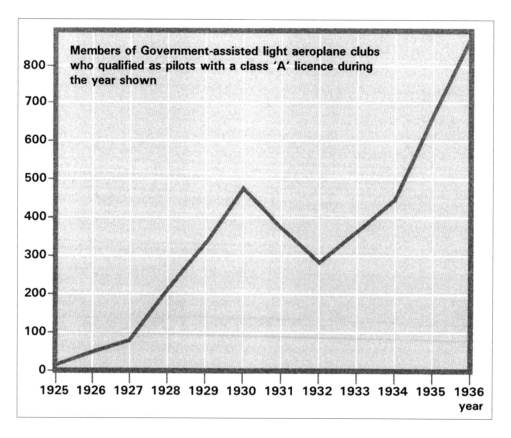

A Morris Motors' promotional illustration depicting a 1931 Morris Major Six Saloon, with a folding head, standing alongside a de Havilland Cirrus Moth.

Despite being rejected, Wolseley continued to approach the Air Ministry from time to time with a desire to develop a type of engine to suit the Ministry's requirements. Eventually the Air Ministry responded and in a letter sent on 28 March, 1935, Wolseley were advised that:

> except for one [of the four engine firms already under contract], which also relies on civil work, it is a matter of the greatest difficulty to provide them with enough work to keep them employed. It is very unlikely, therefore, that anything can be done to consider any engine of your design for Royal Air Force purposes.[3]

Wolseley's persistent efforts to interest the Air Ministry in their products had, therefore, come to nothing as Wolseley was not one of the established aero engine manufacturers with whom the Ministry already had contracts – Rolls-Royce Ltd, The Bristol Aeroplane Co. Ltd, Armstrong-Siddeley Motors Ltd and D. Napier & Sons Ltd.

Four months later, the case was taken up by Lord Nuffield himself when, on 25 July 1935, he wrote to the Air Minister, Lord Swinton (then Sir Philip Cunliffe-Lister), as follows:

> I have to be in London next Wednesday, July 31st, and I should very much like to call and have a short talk with you during that day at some time convenient to yourself. Perhaps I should mention that it is not my intention to ask for anything apart from your advice.
>
> Possibly you are aware that for the last six years one of my companies, Wolseley Motors of Birmingham, has undertaken the development and manufacture of aircraft engines. The work has now reached a stage at which production can be undertaken, and a new company has recently been formed in connection with this enterprise called Wolseley Aero Engines.
>
> During the past year or so Mr W. Cannell, managing director of this company, has done all he can to interest the Air Ministry, but up to now he has been unsuccessful. It is this point on which I should like to have your advice as it occurs to me that if there is no

prospect of our doing business with the Ministry, it would perhaps be wiser to liquidate the company and abandon our aero engine activities altogether.[4]

Lord Swinton (1884–1972) replied to Lord Nuffield on 29 July, saying:

> I have just seen your letter of the 25th, and I am sorry to say that it will be quite impossible for me to see you on Wednesday. I have two Cabinet Committees as well as a Cabinet, and two deputations, and I have to be in the House and to attend a public dinner, so that literally every minute of my time is taken up. You will, I am sure, appreciate that at the end of the Session there is a most tremendous rush.[5]

Lord Swinton had only taken office on 7 June 1935 and was overwhelmed with work, so it was quite understandable that he should put off such a request. However, his somewhat curt letter did not offer an alternative date for an interview or even the possibility of a distant one, and it ignored Lord Nuffield's specific request for advice. Lord Nuffield felt that he had been snubbed and said, 'This is the first time in my life that I have ever been turned down by a Cabinet Minister';[6] it was the start of a long drawn out dispute.

Reviewing the event some sixteen months later, *The Aeroplane* commented:

> …the antipathetic temperaments of a highly successful and very wealthy industrialist and a Minister of His Majesty's Cabinet seem to have generated a critical temperature between them. Lord Nuffield has been accustomed to dictate, and without the faculty for and insistence on dictation he would probably never have achieved his phenomenal success. His patriotism is not in doubt, but very obviously he wished to contribute to the national need either on his own terms or at a rate to set decided limits on the degree of subordination to which he was prepared to submit. On the Government side, Lord Nuffield seems to have been treated with rather less tact due to a great industrial power and when once the hackles had begun to rise on both sides the personalities involved precluded the necessary degree of give and take.[7]

Lord Swinton passed Lord Nuffield's letter to Lord Weir, an adviser to the Air Minister from 1935 to 1938, and Weir noted:

> Personally I think that this is one of the cases where a powerful company have attempted aero-engine development and they have taken the civil field as a starting point. So far as I know, their engines are of insufficient power for service machines, other than training types. As you know, I consider the four existing firms constitute an ample structure for supplying the engines for our existing programme. My visit to Rolls-Royce strengthens me in this view. Unless Nuffield is prepared to continue to fight in the civil field and win through in that field, then any spare facilities which he possesses in his aero department could, of course, carry out subcontracting for the existing firms.[8]

Lord Weir (1877–1959) had a very chequered career in the field of aero engines. He was a Scottish engineering businessman who, as Sir William Weir, had been the director general of Aircraft Production in 1917. So that he could become the Air Minister, Weir was made a peer in April 1918 and, soon after his appointment, he was persuaded that the ABC Dragonfly nine-cylinder, radial engine would reliably give its estimated performance of 340hp for a weight of 600lb, even though it had not been fully developed or tested.

The simplicity of the Dragonfly made Weir believe that it would be easy to manufacture in quantity so contracts were awarded to seventeen firms for sixty experimental engines (Wolseley received a contract for twelve) and 10,700 production engines. At the same time, instructions were given to manufacturers to stop making most other types of aero engines so they could standardise on the mass production of the Dragonfly.

Lord Swinton.

Many new types of aircraft were designed to accept the Dragonfly, but its development ran into serious problems. In addition the engine was both overweight and underpowered. Despite urgent action taken by the Royal Aircraft Establishment to redesign the cylinder heads and to cure a severe vibration, which could cause the crankshaft and other components to fracture, production of the engine was delayed. By December 1918, only twenty-three Dragonfly engines had been delivered and, when the Establishment realised the error of their ways, its production was abandoned. The signing of the Armistice in November 1918 inevitably saved the RAF from the consequences of Lord Weir's decision.

The debacle that surrounded the ABC Dragonfly doubtless influenced Lord Weir and made him exercise extreme caution when he advised the Air Minister about Wolseley aero engines because, at that time, these engines were not yet fully proven.

On 19 November 1935, nearly four months after their exchange of correspondence, Lord Nuffield must have been surprised when he received the following letter from Lord Swinton:

> You will remember suggesting to me in July that we should discuss the question of aero-engines, and I was very sorry that at the time I was so pre-occupied with new work here that I was unable to meet you on the day which you suggested. After I first took over, my urgent work was to arrange for the execution of the new programme, which necessarily depended on certain specified types of machines and engines. In all this, as you know, I have had the constant help of Lord Weir. This programme has occupied us both to the full, but we are now able to look further ahead, and we should very much like to have a talk with you at this stage. Would it be convenient for you to meet us on Wednesday, the 27th November? I have provisionally arranged with Weir to keep the time from three o'clock onwards that day free.[9]

At the meeting Lord Nuffield and William Cannell were received by Lord Swinton himself along with Lord Weir and Air Marshall Sir Hugh Dowding, who was then Air Member for Research and Development. No doubt reflecting his concern over the fact that Germany was known to be rearming, Lord Nuffield opened his remarks by expressing 'his anxiety about the unpreparedness of the supply arrangements for the production of aero-engines'.[10] Lord Nuffield opined, using his experience of mass production and careful cost controls, that the price the Air Ministry was already paying for aero engines was too high and he asked whether it was of any use going on with the development of Wolseley aero engines, because of the lack of support he was getting from the Air Ministry. Dowding explained that the Wolseley engines were, at first, too small although the 600hp Gemini engine, which was then under development, just came within the lower end of the military range. The Air Ministry 'had promised, in spite of certain difficulties, to provide an aircraft in which the Gemini could be tested for endurance purposes in the air. Lord Nuffield and William Cannell both acknowledged the Ministry's assistance in this respect…'.[11]

Lord Swinton and Lord Weir then described the structure of the aero engine industry and outlined the situation concerning the Air Ministry's expansion programme to increase the number of first-line and reserve aircraft for the RAF, in order to maintain parity with the rate of German air rearmament:

> They explained that the programme was within the capacity of the existing industry, and the production of reserves on the scale then anticipated, after this programme was complete, was probably also within capacity. Both [Lord Swinton] and Lord Weir, however, gave it as their personal opinion that the introduction of a fifth engine firm, if that firm was a large motor manufacturing concern, would be welcome on the ground of the production experience which it could contribute.

Nevertheless:

> …at the same time they made it clear to Lord Nuffield that the real customer for the military aero-engine was the aeroplane manufacturer and that an engine market could not be guaranteed by the Air Ministry, although in certain circumstances the Air Ministry had intervened to encourage aeroplane manufacturers to adopt a certain type of engine.[12]

An ABC Dragonfly aero engine built by Wolseley Motors Ltd in 1918.

Sir Hugh Dowding.

Realising that Wolseley aero engines were not wanted, Lord Nuffield offered to acquire a licence, at his own expense, to make American Pratt & Whitney aero engines, or any other engine that was required, but his offers were refused with a comment from Lord Swinton, 'That is your business.'[13] Lord Weir pointed out that Lord Nuffield's suggestion, 'would not be an attractive proposal to the Royal Air Force' and continued, 'it was most desirable to keep to British types, which were proved and wholly satisfactory and what would be required in any further expansion would be a larger programme of British types, which would fit in with the aeroplane programme.'[14] 'On being told finally that there was nothing he could do, Lord Nuffield picked up his hat and gloves and as he left exclaimed, "God help you in case of war".'[15]

A few days later, on 6 December 1935, the Air Ministry wrote to Wolseley Aero Engines Ltd, confirming:

> that only the most powerful of the engines so far projected by the firm (ie the Gemini) could be considered for use in service aircraft, although there was a possibility that one or more types of civil aircraft employing some lower powered range of Wolseley engines would be chosen for training purposes.[16]

Despite the setback, on 19 December 1935, three weeks after his meeting with the Air Minister, Lord Nuffield wrote personally to Lord Weir saying that he was, 'addressing this letter to you because at that meeting it was yourself and not the Air Minister who gave us a measure of encouragement for the future'. He went on to say that he intended to go abroad for about four months early in the new year (Lord Nuffield was in the habit of making annual sea voyages to visit Morris Distributors and Dealers in Australia and the other Dominions) and that while he was away he hoped that Lord Weir would have a discussion with William Cannell on the '...future of our aero engine activities'.

He continued:

> If it appears from the talk that there is a genuine prospect of our being of service, we shall probably continue our developments, but if not, I shall have no alternative but to bring the venture to a close and liquidate the company in the certainty that I will not at any future time undertake the manufacture of aeroplane engines.[17]

The letter apparently got lost for three weeks and was not answered until 9 January, 1936, when Lord Weir wrote to Lord Nuffield and offered to meet William Cannell later that month. By this time Lord Nuffield was on board ship en route to Australia, so his secretary replied saying she would give him Weir's letter when he returned at the beginning of May. On his return to Britain, Lord Nuffield discovered that his request to Lord Weir had not been fulfilled and that the Air Ministry had initiated the Shadow Factory scheme to manufacture aero engines. He also found that several motor firms, who were to manage the shadow factories, had set up a committee to liaise with the Air Ministry and had appointed Sir Herbert Austin, then aged seventy, as chairman.

Lord Nuffield's discontent with the Air Ministry deepened. It was a situation which did not bode well for the future.

Notes

1   *Morris Owner*, March 1934, pp.50–54.
2   *The Aeroplane*, 28 October 1936, p.526.
3   Ibid.
4   Ibid.
5   Ibid.
6   Ibid.
7   *The Aeroplane*, 28 October 1936, p.527.
8   Reader, W.J., p.257.
9   CMD 5295, p.4.
10 Ibid.
11 CMD 5295, p.5.
12 CMD 5295, p.4.
13 Leasor, James, p.142.
14 CMD 5295, p.5. According to *The Aeroplane*, 28 October 1936, p.526, Lord Nuffield sent engineers to the United States, sometime after the meeting, to investigate the latest production methods in case the Air Ministry changed its mind.
15 Andrews and Brunner, p.220.
16 CMD 5295, p.6.
17 Montgomery Hyde, H., p.373.

5

THE SHADOW FACTORY SCHEME

One day in September 1935, Roy Fedden of the Bristol Aeroplane Co. visited Air Marshall Sir Hugh Dowding, Air Member for Research and Development, to argue the case for a British supply of modern variable-pitch or constant-speed propellers. The talk ranged far and wide, then, suddenly, Dowding said:

> Look here Fedden, I think you will be relieved to learn that the Air Staff have come to the conclusion that we are going to have a war with Germany. Quite when it will come we cannot say; it may not be for ten years. But what we must do as soon as we can is precisely what you have been advocating, and that is to build up a vast increase in our production potential… What we have decided to do is to choose an established manufacturer and then try to create a replica of his production process elsewhere. We have called the technique 'Shadowing', because it aims to create a second image of the original… Of course there is no reason why the Shadow should not be much larger than the original, but at present we merely have authority to choose our manufacturer and open negotiations. We have chosen you. Bristol engines are essentially simple, and easily made by standard machine tools and equipment. What also counted very heavily with us was your great experience in licence agreements with many foreign firms. We are convinced that with Bristol engines of established types we are minimising the risk in launching this bold procedure.[1]

So, even though the Air Ministry had advised Lord Nuffield at the end of November 1935 that the existing aircraft industry could cope with the expansion programme, it had already become apparent that the so-called Shadow Factory scheme, originally designed to be set up and then kept on a care and maintenance basis until the actual outbreak of war, would have to be brought into operation as soon as possible to provide additional manufacturing capacity.[2] It also became evident that the Air Ministry needed to strengthen its staff, to monitor the production progress in both the aircraft and Shadow Industries, and so the Directorate of Aeronautical Production was set up in March 1936, under Lt-Col. H.A.P. Disney.[3]

The Government Shadow Factory scheme involved the manufacture of both airframes and aero engines but, as this account concerns aero engines, only that part of the Shadow Factory scheme will now be recounted.

The expansion of aero engine manufacturing facilities was planned to be carried out in two ways:

First: those companies which were already producing aero engines for the Air Ministry – Rolls-Royce, Bristol, Armstrong-Siddeley and Napier – would have their plants extended.

THE BRISTOL AEROPLANE CO., LTD.   FILTON, BRISTOL   This advertisement appeared in July 1936.

Second: a number of Shadow Factories would be built to mass produce, initially, some 4,000 Bristol Mercury and Pegasus radial aero engines (the Pegasus is a long stroke version of the Mercury) within two or three years, independent of continuing output by the Bristol Aeroplane Co. The new production capacity would also provide spare capacity in the event of war after the 4,000 engines had been built.

Having taken the decision to activate the Shadow Factory scheme, Lord Swinton began a series of interviews with the leaders of seven motor manufacturers by seeing Sir Herbert Austin, who was then aged sixty-nine, on 28 February 1936. These motor manufacturers had been allocated to the Air Ministry for aero engine production in the event of war, and they were being advised of proposals to set up the Shadow Factory scheme.

On 13 March 1936, a few days after Germany had reoccupied the Rhineland, Lord Swinton and Lord Weir had a meeting with Sir Stanley White, the managing director of the Bristol Aeroplane Co., together with other members of the firm's management, to discuss the Shadow Factory scheme with them. Lord Swinton stressed the scheme was:

> …the only practical way in which the very difficult and dangerous situation prevailing in defence could possibly be rectified. He did not conceal the gravity of the situation or the shortness of time available to reach the very large output [of aero-engines] required. The professional industry must work at its maximum capacity and… the Shadow industry must be brought into being (a) to supplement the deficiencies under the present emergencies, and (b) to learn and be prepared for output in time of war. He wished the Bristol Company to appreciate that in regard to the Shadow industry he was not asking them to undertake a commercial proposition but a piece of national service, and… he was speaking with the full authority of the Government. He asked them to co-operate frankly and wholeheartedly with him and Lord Weir in accomplishing his heavy task.[4]

Above: A Bristol Mercury aero engine.

Right: Sir Herbert Austin, *c.*1929.

Although Sir Stanley White was willing to co-operate with the Air Ministry and the motor manufacturers to establish the Shadow Factory scheme for the production of Bristol aero engines, he had no intention of allowing any company to gain sufficient expertise such that it could set up in competition with Bristol. He told Lord Swinton that his firm's experience, both during the First World War and since:

> pointed unmistakeably to the advantage of dividing the engine among the firms required to produce it. Time would be saved since Bristol would not have to teach each firm how to make the whole engine; the disturbance to the peace-time activities of the Shadow firms would be minimised; and the possibilities of production in war would be much greater. Both Lord Swinton and Lord Weir expressed doubts about this – the former about the possible wartime production delays if one of the firms happened to be bombed, Weir about the time it would take to set up such a complicated scheme – but agreed to raise it with the prospective shadow aero-engine firms.[5]

Soon after this meeting, Lord Swinton followed up his interviews with the leaders of seven motor manufacturers by sending them this letter on 24 March 1936:

> You will be aware of the general policy which the Government intends to pursue in order to ensure that civilian industry may be able to play a prompt and effective part in war production – should that be required – and also to obtain under the present Defence programmes certain supplies which are in excess of the capacity of the normal munitions industries.
>
> Broadly the plan contemplates that a number of firms normally engaged on civil work shall have allotted to them the particular kind of work they will be called upon to undertake in war, that the necessary steps shall be taken to enable such firms to turn over

rapidly to war work in case of need; and that particular firms should be asked during a limited period to produce certain munitions to supplement the output of the regular munitions firms.

It is an essential part of the plan that the ordinary civil work of these firms should not be interfered with, and that the facilities created and put in use in the present emergency shall remain in existence as a 'war potential' when no longer required for current production.

At the Air Ministry I have under consideration the measures to be taken under the above scheme with regard to aero engines. Some actual production of particular types will be required, and plans must also be made for large-scale production in time of war. It is important that the action which is taken to meet temporary requirements should be in accord with the right method to be adopted on a much larger scale in the event of war.

Certain firms have been allocated for the production of aircraft and/or aero-engines in case of war. Your firm is one of these.

Before taking decisions as to the detailed planning of the war potential or the placing of orders for aeroplane engines outside the regular aircraft firms, I am anxious to discuss with firms who will be most directly concerned the best way of achieving the objects set out in paragraph 4.

In particular I would like to have the considered opinion of firms as to whether production of engines on a large scale in war would be best obtained by each firm manufacturing complete engines, or by an arrangement under which selected component parts would be allotted to particular firms with one or more central places of assembly. It will be appreciated that what is required in case of war is rapid production on a large scale of definite approved types. The governing factor is how to get quick large-scale production in such an emergency.'[6]

On 7 April 1936, Lord Swinton and Lord Weir, with Sir Arthur Robinson, chairman of the Supply Board, and other members of the Air Ministry including Major George Bulman, met the leaders of the seven motor manufacturers so that the Government's plans to set up the Shadow Factory scheme could be explained in detail to them. After Lord Swinton had emphasised the urgency of the situation, the motor manufacturers were asked to assist in the production of Bristol aero engines, to meet the needs of the Air Ministry's expansion programme – and to use the opportunity to gain experience in case of war. They were also asked to consider, in conjunction with the Bristol Aeroplane Co., the most practical way to carry out the scheme. Those who were present from the motor firms that day were: Sir Herbert Austin of The Austin Motor Co. Ltd, Douglas Burton of the Daimler Co. Ltd, William Rootes and his brother Reginald of Rootes Securities Ltd, John Black of the Standard Motor Co. Ltd, Spencer Wilks of the Rover Co. Ltd, a representative of Singer & Co. Ltd and William Cannell of Wolseley Aero Engines Ltd.

While the Government was to pay for the erection and equipping of the Shadow Factories, the motor manufacturers were to staff and manage them on the Government's behalf. It was made clear to the motor firms that they were neither being asked to enter the aircraft industry nor being offered a commercial contract and that their work would be for a management fee of £24,000 for the first year, with an additional payment of £75 per engine produced (about £1 million and £3,400, at 2006 values, respectively). After the first year, advances on an agreed scale would be made which would be set off against the management fees earned for the production of engines. The factories would be closed when the expansion of the RAF had been completed and further orders would only be given in the event of a war, when the factories would be reopened.

The leaders of the motor firms agreed to co-operate with the Air Ministry as a team through a committee which they formed at the meeting on 7 April with, as already mentioned, Sir Herbert Austin as chairman. On 21 April 1936, just before Lord Nuffield

William Rootes.

returned to Britain, the Aero-Engine Committee, which now included Leonard Lord who had been transferred from Wolseley in April 1933 to become the managing director of Morris Motors Ltd, reported that they had 'now discussed amongst themselves and with the Bristol Aeroplane Company the best means of carrying out the programme envisaged, and that they were of the opinion that each of the Shadow Factories set up should undertake the manufacture of a different group of parts of aero-engines'.[7] The committee also submitted that final assembly and bench testing of the complete engines should only be undertaken by the Austin Motor Co. Ltd and Wolseley Aero Engines Ltd.

As the Air Ministry preferred that the manufacture of each engine should not be subdivided among as many as seven firms, Lord Swinton suggested that the motor firms should form themselves into two groups, with each group producing complete engines. Accordingly, Sir Herbert Austin agreed, at a meeting held on 30 April 1936, that the committee's proposals should be reconsidered, and a week later, on 7 May, the Air Ministry were advised that, 'the Committee was definitely and unanimously of the opinion that the only safe and practical scheme was for each firm to manufacture one section [of the engines] only'.[8] The committee believed that any other arrangement would require the manufacture of many more jigs and machine tools which would delay the implementation of the scheme, as the same tools would have to be supplied to several different factories. They also argued that the Bristol Aeroplane Co. would face supervision difficulties if several firms made the same components. Lord Swinton resisted any move to reject the committee's recommendations, which were, therefore, accepted. He felt, 'it was a very great achievement to have got the firms to play as a team at all, and he thought [the Government] ought to let them start, at any rate, with the scheme they preferred.'[9]

After he had returned to Britain at the beginning of May 1936, Lord Nuffield expressed his dislike of the Shadow Factory scheme as it seemed to him just a waste of government money to build another factory for Wolseley:

...when he had so recently spent considerable sums on one which was designed for the production of aero-engines, and he was prepared to make them for any price which the government thought suitable.' He also 'thought the shadow industry to be unsound, for the practical reasons that there would be difficulties in the production of parts on this scattered basis, with their producers not being responsible for their assembly, and that if one factory should be put out of action the production of all engines would be hamstrung.[10]

However, another undeclared reason for Lord Nuffield's discontent must surely have been the composition of the Aero-Engine Committee, as it was chaired by his arch rival in the manufacture of motor vehicles, Sir Herbert Austin.

Apparently unaware of the Bristol Aeroplane Co.'s stipulation that no firm should gain sufficient expertise such that it could set up in competition with Bristol, Lord Nuffield instructed William Cannell to write to Lord Weir offering to make complete Bristol engines at Wolseley's existing aero engine factory. Without informing the Aero-Engine Committee, Cannell then sent the following letter on 6 May 1936:

> I am writing to you in regard to the question of our helping the Air Ministry in its present emergency programme. As you are aware, it is proposed that this company should take part in the scheme embracing several other companies in the formation of a shadow organisation for the production of a standard aero engine.
>
> Both Lord Nuffield and I are anxious to help the Air Ministry to increase its production capacity and we, therefore, propose, for your attention and due consideration, that we shall undertake to manufacture complete Bristol aero-engines in quantities up to 2,000 at a price equal to that at present being paid by the Air Ministry to the Bristol Company.
>
> We are an established aero-engine company equipped with the very latest plant and inspection machinery which can be quickly duplicated, and we can commence deliveries of two or three Bristol engines per week in approximately six months time. It is our considered opinion that this company, by rendering the service we have suggested, would be of greater value to the Air Ministry than by co-operating in the shadow organization scheme.[11]

Lord Weir referred the letter to the Air Council and three weeks later Cannell received the following negative reply from Sir Christopher Bullock, the Permanent Secretary to the Air Ministry:

Lord Nuffield.

At the meeting on April 7th, at which you represented the Wolseley Company, the policy on which the Ministry had decided was fully explained to the representatives, and the seven firms undertook to form themselves into a committee to submit a scheme to carry out that policy.

That policy, as you recall, had two objects - to provide an organisation by which the motor firms concerned could turn over rapidly to war production in case of emergency, and to secure an additional output of aero-engines for the Air Force expansion programme beyond the professional aero-engine industry.

It was expressly stated that there was no intention of interfering with the existing commercial work of the firms or to invite new companies to enter into the list of professional firms to supply aero-engines for the Royal Air Force, and that after the period of expansion no Air Ministry orders could be given to the shadow firms excepting in the case of emergency.

The proposals made in your letter of May 6th appear to be completely at variance with this policy.

Whatever success may be achieved by your company in the production of engines during the expansion period, the scheme would contribute little towards the development of the largely extended capacity required for an emergency, nor would there be created thereby any prospect of Air Ministry's orders for engines from your company after the expansion was completed.

The Council understood that your firm was co-operating with the six other automobile firms to produce a single team to further the shadow scheme for which the Committee have now made definite proposals and which it is the policy of the Air Ministry to adopt.

For these reasons the Council are unable to entertain the scheme you now suggest.[12]

In response to this, Lord Nuffield is reported to have said later:

I am asked to put up a Shadow Factory at Government expense when I already have an aero-engine factory standing there doing nothing. If that's not a waste of public money, then I don't know what is. It's incredible to me. I even offered to build parts in my factory. No, it must be in an Air Ministry factory. Perhaps they imagine I can't make pistons. It's staggering. Really, you can hardly conceive that such a state of things exist. I don't understand it, and I don't suppose anyone else will, either.[13]

By supplying complete Bristol aero engines for the same price as that already being paid by the Air Ministry, rather than assembling these engines within the Shadow Factory scheme on a management-fee basis, Lord Nuffield would not only have received a return on the large amount of money that he had already invested in setting up Wolseley's aero engine factory, but he would also have obviated the need to collaborate with a committee chaired by Sir Herbert Austin.

On 16 June 1936, Lord Nuffield had another interview with Lord Weir, during which he:

… expressed concern at the fact that he did not know how best the production facilities of his company could be utilised. He asked that representatives of the Ministry should meet Mr. Lord and examine the general facilities of the Morris and Wolseley Companies and discuss the best way of using these facilities in peace and in war.'[14] Accordingly, Lt-Col.. H.A.P. Disney, the Air Ministry's Director of Aeronautical Production, visited Wolseley's factory and, 'in the course of a conversation with Mr. Lord, he gathered that while Wolseley would be prepared to participate in the scheme worked out by the Aero-Engine Committee, they would greatly prefer to make whole engines instead of components only.[15]

Leonard P. Lord.

Being a member of this committee, Leonard Lord was clearly opposed to Lord Nuffield's views concerning the Shadow Factory scheme and in making such a statement was seemingly acting without Lord Nuffield's authority.

Partly as a result of Disney's report on his discussion with Leonard Lord, representatives of the seven motor firms met Lord Swinton and Lord Weir again on 29 June 1936. At the meeting, Lord Swinton reminded the representatives of the objectives of the Shadow Factory scheme and asked them to confirm their willingness to participate in it. This was to ensure that there were no misunderstandings before a meeting the following day with the Bristol Aeroplane Co. at Filton, to inspect the components of the type of engine which the motor firms were being asked to make and, at the same time, to determine how its production should be divided amongst them.

Lord Austin, as Sir Herbert had now become,[16] assured Lord Swinton, 'that the whole matter had been most carefully considered' and that 'the committee was still of the opinion the only safe and practical scheme was for each firm to manufacture one section of the aero engines only'. Lord Swinton suggested, 'that some of [the firms] had agreed to adopt the seven-unit scheme only because they thought it was the scheme favoured by the Air Ministry,' and then added, 'It would be a most serious matter if a mistake were made and a unsuitable plan adopted.' In reply, Lord Austin said 'that naturally there was room for differences of opinion amongst the seven firms'. 'Some of them,' he continued, 'including his own company, would, so far as their own interests were concerned, have preferred to make complete engines, but such a course would not have secured the objects in view'.[17]

After the leaders of the motor firms had indicated their agreement with Lord Austin's sentiments, Leonard Lord 'stated that he thought the output required was most likely to be secured by adopting the seven-unit scheme'. 'Specialisation[18] was the simplest and most direct method, but he was not confident that the scheme would succeed and suggested that the Air Ministry should cover itself by obtaining engines from another source as well.' Leonard Lord went on to say 'that though he had little doubt that Wolseley would join the scheme, their participation must for the moment be provisional, as he would need to consult Lord Nuffield'.[19]

The following morning, Leonard Lord had to tell Lord Swinton, by telephone, that 'Lord Nuffield had now decided Wolseley Motors would not co-operate in the Shadow [Factory] scheme'.[20] Lord Swinton, therefore, sent a message to the other members of the Aero-Engine Committee, who were then visiting the Bristol Aeroplane Co., asking them to 'proceed on the basis that Wolseley Motors would not co-operate'.[21] This left only five motor firms in the scheme as the Singer Co. had also dropped out because they did not want to disturb the output of their cars.

To fill the gap left by the withdrawal of Wolseley, the Bristol company themselves agreed to assemble one half of the total output of aero engine sections made by the motor firms, and to bench test them, while the Austin Motor Co. Ltd would undertake this work for the other half as already decided, along with the manufacture of the crankshafts and reduction gears. It was agreed that Bristol's Mercury engine would first be built by the Shadow Factories with the manufacture of the Pegasus to follow at a later date. The committee consented to an output target of fifty aero engines per week and it was determined that each motor firm would expend about 700 man hours on every engine produced. The first fifty sets of all materials would be ordered and distributed by Bristol, to ensure the motor firms started the manufacture of the aero engines with forgings, stampings, castings and other items which were precisely similar to those already used by Bristol.[22]

As close liaison was vital for the future success of the Shadow Factory scheme, members of staff from the motor firms paid frequent visits to Bristol's factory to observe the company's production methods, and Bristol set up a department known as the Shadow Industry Office to supply the necessary technical information. Also, a sub-committee, made up of managers from the respective motor firms, met regularly with personnel from both Bristol's Shadow Industry Office and the Air Ministry to deal with outstanding matters and to progress the scheme. The main co-ordinating role was played by the manager of the Bristol Shadow Industry Office, who was eventually to assume the formal role of co-ordinating engineer.[23]

THE FIRMS INVOLVED IN THE SHADOW FACTORY SCHEME TO MANUFACTURE BRISTOL MERCURY AERO ENGINES

Firm	*Parts Made/Work Undertaken*
The Austin Motor Co.Ltd Longbridge, Birmingham.	Crankshaft and reduction gear. Final engine assembly and test.
Daimler Co. Ltd Coventry.	Crankcase, oil sump, air intake and rocker gear.
Humber Ltd Coventry. (Part of the Rootes Group)	Supercharger and rear cover. Petrol pump.
Standard Motor Co. Ltd Coventry.	Cylinder assemblies.
Rover Co. Ltd Coventry.	Connecting rods, pistons, valves and cam plate.
Bristol Aeroplane Co. Ltd Filton, Bristol.	Final engine assembly and test.

As time went on, Lord Nuffield reconsidered his position and at a meeting on 7 July 1936, requested by Lord Austin, Leonard Lord advised Lord Weir that if the Air Ministry bought from Morris Motors Ltd a building in Coventry[24] to use as a Shadow Factory, Wolseley would re-enter the Shadow Factory scheme. The following day, Lord Weir discussed this

proposal with both Lord Nuffield and Leonard Lord, and when the offer was refused Lord
Nuffield told Lord Weir that 'he did not want to take part in the Shadow [Factory] scheme
but it had his entire good will.'[25]

Shortly after the discussion, 'the Aero-Engine Committee approached Wolseley Motors with
a proposition that they should take over the manufacture of certain sections, together with the
erecting and testing part of the engines.'[25] On 7 August 1936, Leonard Lord, who was apparently
once again acting without Lord Nuffield's authority, telephoned Lt-Col. Disney, saying that:

> Wolseley Motors Ltd were definitely coming into the [Shadow Factory] scheme, and after
> again suggesting that the Air Ministry should take over the factory referred to previously,
> agreed to establish a [Shadow] factory in Birmingham. An officer of the Directorate of
> Aeronautical Production accordingly visited Birmingham to make detailed arrangements
> with the firm, and in a letter dated 14th August 1936, Mr. Lord submitted full proposals for
> the erection and equipment of the factory.[26]

Although Lord Nuffield and Leonard Lord held opposing views about Wolseley's entry
into the Shadow Factory scheme, over which neither would give way to the other, these
differences came to an abrupt end when Lord Nuffield discovered Leonard Lord had been
indiscreet with a female member of the office staff at the Cowley factory. As a result, Leonard
Lord was obliged to resign from his position as managing director of Morris Motors Ltd on
24 August 1936. The often recounted story about the reason for Leonard Lord's resignation
being his discontent with the level of his salary is probably a 'red herring' to disguise the
truth. In any case, the profits of over £2 million (about £88 million at 2006 values) generated by the Nuffield Organizations in 1936, would have given Leonard Lord substantial
bonus payments, bearing in mind that Lord Nuffield was known to be generous to his staff.
Although the level of Leonard Lord's salary has not been found, some indication can be

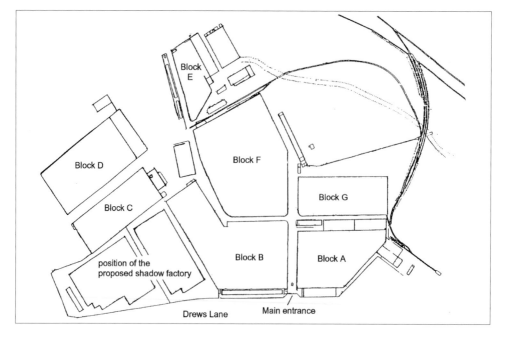

A plan of Wolseley's factory at Ward End, Birmingham. The two buildings of the proposed
Shadow Factory for the production of Bristol aero engines were never erected. Wolseley radial
aero engines were manufactured in Block G.

Harry Seaward.

gathered from the ledgers of Morris Industries Ltd. These show that in the twelve months between October 1935 and September 1936, T.C. Skinner, the managing director of the S.U. Carburetter Co. (a business bought by Lord Nuffield in 1927), received £6,067 2s 4d in salary and bonuses, which equates to £265,000 at 2006 values. Being of a more senior position, Leonard Lord would inevitably have earned a greater amount.

Soon after they had agreed to part company, Lord Nuffield sent for Leonard Lord and said, 'Now that you're leaving me, Len, I want you to take this with you', and he handed him a cheque for £50,000 (about £2.25 million at 2006 values). At first, Leonard Lord refused the offer and said, '… I can't take it. I'll take the usual compensation if you like, but I can't take £50,000 from you', to which Lord Nuffield replied, 'Len, if you don't take it, I'll never speak to you again. Our friendship will be over'.[27]

It had been three years since Lord Nuffield had transferred Leonard Lord from Wolseley Motors Ltd in Birmingham to Morris Motors Ltd at Cowley, which he transformed into the largest and technically most modern vehicle manufacturing plant in Europe, capable of making 2,000 vehicles a week and with record levels of pre-tax profits.

Nevertheless, there is some evidence to suggest Leonard Lord had not been popular at the Cowley factory, as soon after his arrival, Miles Thomas, who was then director and general sales manager of Morris Motors Ltd, accepted an offer to become the general manager of Morris Commercial Cars Ltd in Birmingham, because, '… life wasn't the same as it had been before LPL [Leonard Lord] took over.' Thomas continued:

> …when LPL splurged into the Cowley scene [in 1933] he awoke people to the hard facts of life. Most of them had never worked anywhere else except Cowley and were stiff in their attitudes. He swiftly made them flexible. Everyone admired his methods if not his manners… He walked roughly over the toes of anyone who got in his way. LPL and I did not altogether see eye to eye. My philosophy was always to persuade people. Len's was a far more forceful approach.[28]

Amongst Lord Nuffield's papers there is a handwritten letter, dated 22 June 1936, from his secretary, Wilfred Hobbs, to Andrew Walsh, Lord Nuffield's solicitor and legal advisor. The letter concerns Harry Seaward who had been a director of Morris Motors Ltd since 1927 and who had replaced Miles Thomas at Cowley as general sales manager in 1934. Hobbs wrote that he had had a conversation with Seaward '…on the subject of his future in the event of Lord Nuffield's passing out'. He went on to say that Seaward:

> …is rather worried because he knows he is not persona grata with the Managing Director [Leonard Lord] and supposes, correctly I think, that if such an occurrence did arise he

would be speedily invited to pass in his checks. I have mentioned the matter to Lord
Nuffield who is sympathetic but, like me, is a bit hazy as to how to arrange protection...

The letter is significant because not only is it clear that Leonard Lord was having a dispute
with Seaward, about which neither Hobbs nor Lord Nuffield apparently agreed, but it also
gives some background on the difficult relationships that had built up between Leonard
Lord and the senior management at Cowley.

On his return from a holiday in the USA, following his resignation, Leonard Lord
remarked, 'I am pigheaded and Lord Nuffield has his opinions. There was no row between
us. A few minutes after we had decided to break our business relations we had a gin and
french together, and we laughed over the fact we could sit drinking, although we had taken
a step that grieved us both.'[29] The pair, however, were soon together again as five months
after their break, in February 1937, Leonard Lord accepted an offer from Lord Nuffield
to administer a £2 million trust fund to aid areas of high unemployment in Britain – an
assignment he undertook until 15 December 1937 for a monthly salary of £416 3s 4d
(£5,000pa, about £210,000 at 2006 values) drawn from Lord Nuffield's own funds.

According to Lord Swinton, '[Leonard] Lord generously offered, if [the Air Ministry]
decided to have another [Shadow] factory built in place of the [Wolseley] one, that he
would undertake its management.' He continued, 'I very much wanted Lord in the aircraft
picture, but we came to the conclusion that if he were agreeable we could use him elsewhere, and we arranged that he should join Austins to take charge both of the airframe
production and of the engine and assembly work which that firm was to undertake.'[30]

So in February 1938, with apparent encouragement from the Air Minister, Leonard
Lord, who was then forty-one, joined the Austin Motor Co. at Longbridge, as works director, and not only became a rival to Lord Nuffield in the manufacture of motor vehicles
but also took up a position on the Aero-Engine Committee once again – but this time
working for a different motor firm.

The job of withdrawing Leonard Lord's offer to the Air Ministry for the setting up of a
factory at Wolseley to replace Bristol in the Shadow Factory scheme, fell upon Oliver Boden
who had succeeded Leonard Lord at Morris Motors Ltd and was now Lord Nuffield's deputy. Accordingly, Boden sent a letter to Lt-Col. Disney on 26 August 1936, two days after
Leonard Lord had resigned, saying that, 'owing to a change of management his company
wished to withdraw the proposals contained in Mr. Lord's letter of the 14th August'.[31] On
receipt of the letter, Disney telephoned Boden and asked him to come to the Air Ministry to
explain the situation. No doubt recalling how Lord Nuffield had been treated when he had
requested a meeting with Lord Swinton a year earlier, Boden said that he could not come
for ten days but Disney was emphatic and told him that he must come that afternoon, to
which he conceded. At the meeting, Boden explained to Sir Cyril Newall, the Air Member
for Supply and Organisation, that, 'in view of the amount of reorganisation which was taking
place in Morris Motors Ltd. he could not, in fairness to the Air Ministry, continue with the
Shadow Scheme and do justice to it'.[32] In some desperation, the Air Ministry immediately
got in touch with the Bristol Aeroplane Co. and during an interview with one of their representatives that same afternoon, it was again agreed that Bristol would replace Wolseley in the
Shadow Factory scheme. Although the dispute between Lord Nuffield and the Air Ministry
had reached its climax, it was not the end of the story because Lord Nuffield publicly vented
his feelings at a press conference two months later, as outlined in Chapter Seven.

The task of erecting and equipping the vast new Shadow Factories in Coventry and
Birmingham for the manufacture of Bristol Mercury and Pegasus aero engines, commenced apace during the summer of 1936. 'There was magnificent collaboration and
mutual goodwill between [the five motor firms that remained in the scheme], spiced with
healthy rivalry',[33] although once production had started, the Shadow industry was not
without its problems – sometimes due to communication failures and sometimes due to

delays in the supply of components. Also, some supercharger assemblies proved to be unreliable because William Rootes had decided to defy the advice of both Bristol and Major George Bulman of the Air Ministry, to use only Swiss Maag grinders for the manufacture of the supercharger's gear wheels. Humber Ltd (a company within the Rootes Group), therefore, bought British Orcutt gear-grinding equipment as well and as a consequence, when the first Shadow-built Bristol Mercury VIII aero engines fitted with Orcutt-ground gears started their 100-hour type test during the early part of 1938, the 'gears broke up at about forty hours running, wrecking the engine'.[34]

'Bulman was very angry indeed, confirmed that no Shadow gear [wheels] could be trusted beyond 10 hours, and ordered an immediate switch to [Bristol's] method [of manufacture].'[35] The upshot was a shortage of superchargers while Humber resolved the situation so the Shadow Factories were, therefore, unable to meet their output target of seventy-five aero engines per week until October 1938. (The target weekly output of aero engines had been raised from fifty to seventy-five in March 1938.) By then, the reliability of the engines had improved and three months later, in December 1938, 'when most of the Mercuries in the RAF's Blenhiem squadrons were Shadow-built, one of these engines and a duplicate made at Bristol were stripped, shuffled together and re-assembled'.[36] The successful outcome of this operation enabled Lord Austin to write to Lord Swinton as follows:

> I thought you would be interested to hear about the following in view of the fact that the possibility of the Scheme of Shadow Factories being a success was so much decried in certain quarters when it was first put into force. A test was made by the Bristol Aeroplane Company of two engines, viz. one built entirely by the Bristol Aeroplane Company (not in their Shadow Factory) and an engine which was assembled by the Bristol Aeroplane Company out of parts manufactured by Members of the Shadow Group.
>
> The two engines were totally dismantled, the parts mixed up together, and re-assembled and put on test. The test was entirely satisfactory, proving that the work done by the Shadow Group was quite equal to the work being done by the Bristol Aeroplane Company in their normal manufacture. In other words, the parts were interchangeable, justifying the Shadow scheme '100 per cent'.[37]

W.E. Rootes, managing director of Rootes Securities Ltd, left, and Lt-Col. J.A. Cole, chairman of the Humber Ltd, centre, inspecting the supercharger unit for a Bristol Mercury aero engine. (*Aeroplane*/www. aeroplanemonthly.com)

This page: Four views showing the manufacture of Bristol Mercury aero engines at The Austin Motor Co. Ltd, Longbridge, Birmingham. The initial and final assembly of these engines can be seen to be taking place in two underground tunnels, as a precaution against enemy bombing. These tunnels, which were 60ft below the surface, were 776ft long, 16ft wide and 10ft high.

Above: Assembling the reduction gears.

Left: Machining and inspecting the crankshafts.

Initial assembly of the split crankcase.

Final assembly of the aero engines.

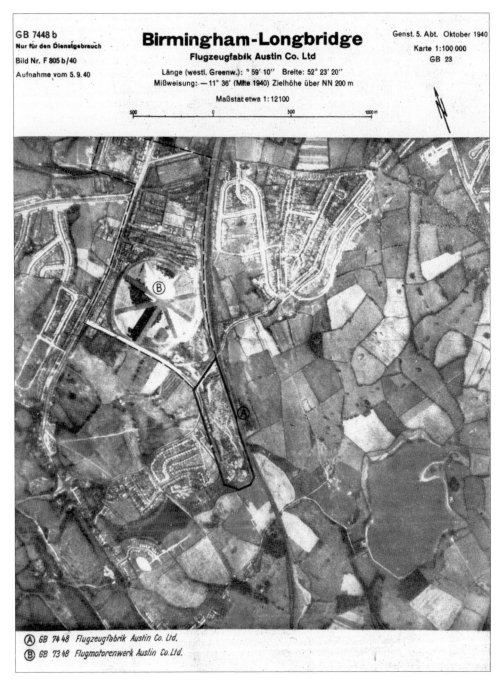

GB 7448 b
Nur für den Dienstgebrauch
Bild Nr. F 805 b/40
Aufnahme vom 5. 9. 40

Birmingham-Longbridge
Flugzeugfabrik Austin Co. Ltd

Länge (westl. Greenw.): ° 59' 10''   Breite: 52° 23' 20''
Mißweisung: —11° 36' (Mtte 1940) Zielhöhe über NN 200 m

Maßstat etwa 1:12100

Genst. 5. Abt. Oktober 1940
Karte 1:100 000
GB 23

Ⓐ GB 7448 *Flugzeugfabrik Austin Co. Ltd.*
Ⓑ GB 7348 *Flugmotorenwerk Austin Co. Ltd.*

This German reconnaissance photograph of the Austin Motor Co.'s factory at Longbridge, Birmingham, was taken on 5 September 1940, a few weeks before the factory was bombed with the loss of six lives and twenty-five injured. Area 'A' shows the Shadow Factory for the construction of airframes whereas area 'B' accommodates the circular flying ground, the vehicle test track and the north, south and west sections of the motor works, which are wrongly described as an aero engine factory (Flugmotorenwerk). In fact, the underground aero engine factory, shown on page 98, was located at the north end of area 'A'. The Bristol Road and Lowhill Lane can be seen running along the eastern and southern sides of area 'B', respectively.

On 22 July 1938, Sir Kinsley Wood, the Air Minister, visited Austin's Shadow Factory at Longbridge, Birmingham, and he is seen here inspecting an Austin-built Bristol Mercury aero engine with Lord Austin, who was then aged seventy-two. Also seen, from right to left, are: N. Rowbotham, production director of the Bristol Aeroplane Co., L.P. Lord, works director of the Austin Motor Co., Lt-Col. H.A.P. Disney, the Air Ministry's director of production, and, almost hidden behind Lord Austin, Mr Ledgard, works manager of Austin's Shadow Factory. (*Aeroplane*/www.aeroplanemonthly.com)

Undoubtedly, the output of aero engines from the Shadow industry made an indispensable contribution to the expansion of Britain's air strength immediately before and during the Second World War. At the end of the war, the Shadow Factories which were making Bristol Mercury and Pegasus engines (another Shadow Factory scheme was set up in 1939 to make Bristol Hercules engines) were turning out some 800 engines a month so Lord Nuffield's fears about the viability of the scheme proved to be unfounded. However, to mitigate the effects of enemy bombing, the assembly of Bristol aero engines at Austin's Longbridge factory was carried out in underground workshops while the Air Ministry acquired and adapted all sorts of premises, such as 'old skating rinks, cinemas, warehouses and barns... to receive machinery and services'[38] so that parallel lines of manufacture could be provided if necessary. Nevertheless, it was fortunate that enemy action against the Shadow Factories turned out to be relatively small and did not cause any serious interruption of output.

Whatever the reasons for Lord Nuffield's failure to co-operate in the Shadow Factory scheme:

> ...the reputation of having prevented the Government from taking advantage of Nuffield's services stuck to Swinton; and it was significant that just three days after he had succeeded him as Air Minister, Kingsley Wood saw Nuffield and arranged for him to build the largest of all the Shadow Factories at Castle Bromwich to produce, not aero-engines, but Spitfire air frames.[39]

(See Chapter Nine for details of Lord Nuffield's involvement with Castle Bromwich Aircraft Factory.)

Notes

1   Gunston, Bill, p.82.
2   The idea of supplementing the production of the armament industries on the outbreak of war by the output of factories already established, at Government expense, by other technically related industries, such as the motor industry, had been adumbrated as early as 1927, and a paper on the subject by Lord Weir was approved in principle by the Committee of Imperial Defence at the end of May 1934. See Cross, J.A., p.160.
3   Richie, Sebastion, pp.46, 47.
4   Reader, W.J., p.262.
5   Cross, J.A., p.162.
6   CMD 5295, pp.12, 13.
7   CMD 5295, p.9.
8   CMD 5295, p.9.
9   Cross, J.A., p.163.
10 Andrews & Brunner, p.221.
11 *The Aeroplane*, 28 October 1936, p.526.
12 *The Aeroplane*, 28 October 1936, p.527.
13 Leasor, James, pp.140, 141.
14 CMD 5295, pp.9, 10.
15 Ibid.
16 Sir Herbert Austin was created a Baron in 1936, taking the title Lord Austin of Longbridge.
17 CMD 5295, p.10.
18 The word 'specialisation' was used by Morris Motors Ltd at that time to promote their method of vehicle production, such that some factories within the Morris Motors group were 'specialised' in the manufacture of certain components.
19 CMD 5295, p.10.
20 CMD 5295, pp.10, 11.
21 Ibid.
22 Bulman, George Purvis, p.226.
23 Richie, Sebastian, p.125.
24 This building was probably in Gosford Street, Coventry, which, in 1936, was being vacated by Morris Motors Ltd, Engines Branch as they were moving into a new, purpose-built factory at Courthouse Green, Coventry. Throughout the Second World War the Gosford Street factory was occupied by Nuffield Mechanizations & Aero Ltd for the manufactire of Bofors Guns on behalf of the Government. See Andrews & Brunner, pp.25, 26.
25 Reader, W.J., p.264.
26 CMD 5295, p.11.
27 Jackson, Robert, p.111.
28 Thomas, Sir Miles, pp.172, 173.
29 Leasor, James, pp.68, 69.
30 Viscount Swinton, p.116.
31 CMD 5295, p.11.
32 Ibid.
33 Bulman, George Purvis, p.227.
34 Ibid.
35 Gunston, Bill, p.83.
36 Ibid.
37 Viscount Swinton, p.117.
38 Bulman, George Purvis, p.252.
39 Cross, J.A., p.165.

6

THE TRAGEDY OF AIRSPEED AND WOLSELEY AERO ENGINES

While the negotiations for the setting up of the Shadow Factory scheme were being finalised during the summer of 1936, the Air Ministry became interested in purchasing a quantity of Airspeed Oxford training aircraft fitted with a pair of Wolseley Scorpio engines. Up to then, the Air Ministry had shown little interest in Airspeed's products because the company was not one of the more established aircraft manufacturers and had suffered in a similar way to Wolseley.

Airspeed Ltd had been founded in March 1931 by A. Hessell Tiltman and Nevil Shute Norway, who was to become better known as the author writing under his pen name, 'Nevil Shute'. (Extract from *Slide Rule* by Nevil Shute: 'My full name is Nevil Shute Norway; Nevil Shute is quite a good, euphonious name for a novelist, and Mr Norway could go on untroubled by his other interest and build up a sound reputation as a engineer'.) The company's first airliner, the ten-seat AS4 Ferry bi-plane, was powered by three engines, which were made by de Havilland, one of Airspeed's competitors. Even though the relationship between Airspeed and de Havilland was good, there were obvious commercial disadvantages in using a competitor's products so, being too small to manufacture engines themselves, Airspeed turned their attention to Wolseley as they were an aero engine manufacturer who did not also make aircraft. This was during the winter of 1932/33 and although Wolseley's aero engines were still under development, Airspeed considered these engines to be technically very promising so they began to shape their design policy around them.

The Airspeed Oxford was a development of Airspeed's civil Envoy, a six/eight-seat, low-wing monoplane, the prototype of which registered G-ACMT, first flew on 26 June 1934 in the hands of Flt-Lt C.H.A. Colman.[1] Six days later this aircraft was shown at the Society of British Aircraft Constructors Show at Hendon Aerodrome, and the type received its Certificate of Airworthiness on 9 October 1934. It was powered by a pair of Wolseley Aries A.R.9 radial engines which Airspeed found to be 'small, very quiet and smooth running, with few teething troubles to impeded us',[2] although a modification to the engine's fuel pump spindle had been found necessary after two had sheared during trials. The Envoy had, in turn, been developed from the single-engine Airspeed Courier which had generated much respect for Airspeed as it was the 'first machine to have a practical and reliable retracting undercarriage'.[3]

For test and demonstration purposes, two of the first three Envoys to be built, registered G-ACVH and G-ACVI, during October 1934, were purchased by Wolseley Motors Ltd and by Lord Nuffield himself. While G-ACVH was fitted with Wolseley Aries A.R.9 Mk II engines, Lord Nuffield's own aircraft, G-ACVI, which was named *Miss Wolseley*, had

Right: Nevil Shute.

Below: The prototype Airspeed Envoy, G-ACMT, fitted with a pair of Wolseley A.R.9. Aries, engines cowled with Townend rings. This machine could carry up to eight passengers, with space for luggage, at a cruising speed of 150mph.

Airspeed Envoy G-ACVI, seen under construction. This aircraft, which was purchased by Lord Nuffield in October 1934 and named *Miss Wolseley*, was fitted with a pair of Wolseley, A.R.9. Aries Mark III engines. After being used by Wolseley for test and demonstration purposes, G-ACVI was sold to Ansett Airways of Australia in August 1936, when it was re-registered VH-UXM (see page 110).

Wolseley Aries A.R.9 Mk III engines installed. Among the demonstration and test flights undertaken during its ownership by Lord Nuffield, G-ACVI completed a round trip from England to Cape Town. Piloted by Sqn Ldr E.G. Hilton, G-ACVI took off from Cape Town on 30 May 1936, in an attack on the South Africa to England record but, after being delayed at Athens, Sqn Ldr Hilton lost the possibility of breaking the record.[4] Later, in 1936, G-ACVI was sold to Ansett Airways of Australia and re-registered VH-UXN. Its Wolseley engines apparently performed satisfactorily for the next eight years as in 1944, VH-UXN was re-powered with 350hp Wright Whirlwind seven-cylinder radial engines. By 1945 the aircraft had completed 10,000 hours flying time.

Although only a few of the eighty-two Envoys built were fitted with Wolseley engines, Airspeed's experience convinced them that Wolseley Scorpio engines should power their new AS.10 Oxford, as they considered the 250hp Scorpio to be 'modern in design and with a geared propeller, and a very considerable technical advance on any other British engine in its power range'.[5] Apart from the technical merits of the Scorpio, an insight into its comparatively low cost can be gauged by a quotation Airspeed gave to the Air Ministry in December 1935 for an Envoy. With Armstrong Siddeley Lynx engines, the price quoted was £5,150, whereas the type converted to a trainer and fitted with Wolseley Scorpios would have cost £4,850,[6] a difference of £300 (about £13,500 at 2006 values).

During the negotiations between the Air Ministry and Wolseley Aero Engines Ltd for the supply of Scorpio engines, Wolseley's aero engine sales manager, Mr Richardson, was invited to attend a meeting at the Air Ministry on 20 July 1936, so that he could provide details of the Scorpio. In a confirmation letter sent on 25 July, Wolseley gave 'particulars of the quantities of engines that they were in a position to produce'[7] and eleven days later, on 5 August, the Ministry made a decision to adopt the Scorpio because it 'presented certain advantages'[8] over a competitor's engine. On 11 August Mr Richardson was seen by the Ministry's Assistant Director of Contracts (Engines) who, after explaining the procedure for placing a contract, gave him details of the terms set out in a document entitled 'Instructions to Proceed' (ITP), which the Ministry issued to their contractors. Acting on his own initiative after receiving this information, 'Mr Richardson stated that there would be no difficulty in the acceptance by his company of an Instruction to Proceed on the lines indicated to him.'[9]

Wolseley wasted no time in starting to manufacture the 300 Scorpio engines required by the Air Ministry, and on 19 August 1936:

A Convertible Envoy being packed complete in one crate for shipment to the South African Air Force, at Johannesburg.

7-8 WEEKS

from receipt of order to delivery of first

machine, then one machine each week.

Although during the past year there has

been a rapidly increasing demand for

Airspeed "Envoys" in all parts of the world, deliveries

at this rate can be maintained until further notice.   This

is another fact of importance to airline operators requir-

ing high performance aircraft with 6 or 8 passenger seats.

Executives are invited to write on their letter headings for a copy of the "Airspeed Bulletin" sent free.   To other people who would like a copy, it is sent post free for 6d.

AIRSPEED (1934) LIMITED, THE AIRPORT, PORTSMOUTH, ENGLAND.
Tel.: Portsmouth 2444 (3 lines)

This advertisement
appeared in October 1936.

...the Chief Inspector of Engines in the Aeronautical Inspection Directorate visited the Wolseley works and discussed the problem of output with Mr Cannell. The Chief Inspector was informed that parts were already in production for the first batch of 50 engines and that material supplies were also available for the second batch. A letter confirming the arrangements made was sent to [Wolseley] on 21st August, and was acknowledged by the firm on the 24th. On the same date two members of the staff of the Aeronautical Inspection Directorate were temporarily attached to works.[10]

After trying to get the Air Ministry interested in their products for some two years, Wolseley's staff must have been perplexed when Lord Nuffield made a decision not to supply any Scorpio engines to the Ministry for the Airspeed Oxford, after he had time to consider the terms contained in an ITP. As a result, on 26 August 1936, the same day that he had written to Lt-Col. Disney withdrawing Leonard Lord's offer to join the Shadow Factory scheme, Oliver Boden telephoned the Assistant Director of Contracts (Engines) at the Air Ministry and, 'after saying he understood that Mr. Richardson had discussed the issue of a contract with Wolseley Aero Engines, asked how the matter stood. He was informed that an Instruction to Proceed for the supply of 300 Scorpio engines was either in the post or about to be posted.'[11] (Lord Nuffield apparently received an official ITP the following day, 27 August.) Boden then came to the point and said that a decision had been taken to discontinue the manufacture of aero engines, due to changes that had taken place in the organisation of his company, and that Wolseley's aero engine factory would be closed down the following morning.[12] He did not, apparently, reveal Lord Nuffield's dislike of the terms contained in the ITP which had exacerbated his discontent with the Air Ministry.

So, due to the Air Ministry's bureaucracy, Britain lost a fledgling aero engine manufacturer, owned by a wealthy industrialist who had a great deal of experience with mass production, at a time when European affairs were at a very critical stage. *The Aeroplane*[13] commented:

> One might argue that the types of radial motors on which Wolseley Motors Ltd. must have spent a lot of money during the past three or four years were not enough of an advance on existing types, though very good indeed in their way, to justify bringing yet another type of radial motor into the Air Force. But that seems to be answered by the undisputed fact that 300 Scorpios had been ordered. Whatever may be the inside history of this curious affair the fact remains that the Air Force seems to have lost one of its most valuable potential sources of supply. And as no business man of Lord Nuffield's calibre is going to throw away orders, the assumption, obviously, is that the fault was at the Air Ministry end. Therefore somebody ought to inquire into the affair.

An ITP was issued by the Air Ministry after a manufacturer had quoted a fixed price for a contract. Its purpose was to control the profits of the Air Ministry's contractors to avert criticism from the British electorate and many politicians who were, in 1936, against anything to do with rearmament. Although an ITP enabled a contractor to start work, its terms gave the Air Ministry powers to determine the price the Ministry paid the contractor for its products. The ITP explained that if the Air Minister and the contractor were unable to agree a price, payment would only be made after the Air Minister's representatives had assessed the cost of operating the contractor's business and made an estimate of the overheads concerning the contract. The Air Minister would then determine the price the contractor would be paid, using their 'fixed price' as a maximum but probably paying a much lower figure.

While the aircraft industry was familiar with these terms and had no option but to accept them, this was not the case with the motor industry. According to Nevil Shute, Lord Nuffield and his deputy, Oliver Boden:

> …read [the ITP] carefully, and noted all the provisions; neither of them had seen or heard of anything like it before. If they were to submit their vast business to this sort of an investigation it would mean a wholesale re-orientation of their offices; it would mean engaging an army of chartered accountants on their side with a consequent increase in overheads. They had quoted a price for the engines which might well involve them in a heavy loss, through a genuine sense of patriotism, and they were rewarded by this suspicious nonsense. They were angry. They had spent at that time about two hundred thousand pounds upon the Wolseley aero-engine, and it had only led to this. [From what we now know, the costs of Wolseley's aero-engine project are estimated to have exceeded this amount, as outlined in chapter three]. In the scale of their whole business that was not a large amount of money, and as good business men they knew when to get out of an unsatisfactory venture. To admit the Air Ministry methods of doing business into their vast enterprise would be like introducing a maggot into an apple; the whole thing might well be brought to a ruin in the end. Better to stick to selling motor vehicles for cash to the War Office and the Admiralty who retained the normal methods of buying and selling. They sent the ITP back to the Air Ministry, rejected, and closed down the aero-engine side of their concern.[14]

<u>Instructions to proceed, June, 1935</u>

Fair and reasonable prices shall be paid in repect of _____ items of the schedule. In the event of delay in the settlement of fair and reasonable prices provisional prices will be inserted in the contract by the Secretary of State for the purpose of effecting payment thereunder.

The actual prices to be paid shall if practicable be agreed between the Secretary of State and the Contractor but in the event of disagreement a final settlement shall be deferred until the Contractor has furnished such particulars of costs in connection with the contract as may be required by the Secretary of State and has permitted the same to be verified by a representative of the Secretary of State by inspection of his books. Should any portion of the work under the contract be carried out by a subsidiary or allied firm or company, inspection of the books of such firm or company shall likewise be permitted.

The Secretary of State shall thereafter determine fair and reasonable prices and these shall be the actual prices payable under the contract.

The Secretary of State shall pay such sums as may become due by reason of the actual prices determined as provided for above being in excess of the provisional prices and the Contractor shall refund to the Secretary of State any sums paid on the provisional price in excess of the actual prices.

A sample of the 'Instructions to Proceed' which the Air Ministry issued to their contractors.

Bearing in mind the speed at which the ITP was rejected, coupled with the sudden decision to cease aero engine production, there is, perhaps, another reason for Lord Nuffield's aversion towards the terms contained in the ITP, in addition to those given by Nevil Shute. Wolseley Aero Engines Ltd was owned by Lord Nuffield himself via his holding company Morris Industries Ltd, which not only held all of the shares in the aero engine business but also provided it with finance, as already explained. The entries in the ledgers of Morris Industries Ltd start with a receipt of £2,235,000 on 22 October 1927, and a month later the company received a further £553,309. This money, the total of which equates to about £106 million at 2006 values, had come from the sale of preference shares in Morris Motors Ltd (see Chapter Three) and it enabled Morris Industries Ltd to become the financial hub of the Nuffield Organization, acting as a private bank. In addition to giving financial support to the various companies within the Nuffield Organization, when required, Morris Industries Ltd gave loans/mortgages to individuals, made investments, bought companies and purchased properties, all of which generated a large income. As well as all this, the ledgers of Morris Industries Ltd show many of Lord Nuffield's benefactions, his own drawings, remittances to the Inland Revenue and payments to some of his staff.

Lord Nuffield was a modest person and although he was known to be wealthy, he inevitably did not wish to have his financial affairs and his investments revealed. If the ITP had been accepted, the Air Minister's representatives would probably have demanded to see the ledgers of Morris Industries Ltd, as it financed Wolseley Aero Engines Ltd so the extent of Lord Nuffield's personal financial dealings and his true wealth would have been exposed to a Ministry which had already irritated him over the Shadow Factory scheme. The thought of civil servants 'poking their noses' into the inner workings of his already well controlled business was, undoubtedly, anathema to Lord Nuffield.

Whatever brought about his decision to close down Wolseley's aero engine factory, Lord Nuffield later used the factory to make Nuffield-Liberty tank engines for the War Office in the knowledge that their contracts did not include an ITP

The Air Ministry's practice of issuing an ITP to Wolseley Aero Engines Ltd implied that the company was making excessive profits but Nevil Shute is on record as saying, 'I do not think that even his worst enemy could ever accuse Lord Nuffield of attempting to swindle the British public. The price [Wolseley] quoted struck me as low... on the basis of pounds [£] per horse power it was much lower than the price we were paying for competing engines'. He continued, '[the closure of Wolseley's aero engine business] was a major disaster to Airspeed, for every type [of aircraft] that we were then designing or manufacturing was fitted with a Wolseley engine. It was also a major disaster to Britain, for the [Scorpio] engine was technically far ahead of any competitor in its power range'.[15]

The following Airspeed aircraft were designed to be fitted with Wolseley aero engines:

| AS6 Envoy |) | |
| AS27 Irving biplane |) | Wolseley A.R.9. Aries |

AS6 Envoy	)	
AS7K Military Envoy	)	
AS10 Oxford	)	Wolseley Scorpio
AS27 Irvine biplane	)	
AS30 Wasp	)	
AS34, 12/15 seat, four-engined transport	)	

By this time a new company, Airspeed (1934) Ltd, had been formed with financial backing from the shipbuilders Swann Hunter & Wigham Richardson Ltd. After a hurried consultation with the company's chairman, George Wigham Richardson, Nevil Shute made an urgent visit to see Lord Nuffield at Cowley, whom he found to be very courteous and attentive, to ask if Airspeed could take over the manufacture of Wolseley aero engines. Lord Nuffield told him that 'before closing his aero engine business down he had thought of Airspeed and had ascertained that there was a competing engine that [Airspeed] could use'. Nevil Shute replied that 'it was a rotten engine compared with his', to which Lord Nuffield remarked that, 'for that he had to blame the Air Ministry'. According to Nevil Shute:

> Lord Nuffield was still furious with the Air Ministry. He grew red in the face at the thought of them, thumped the desk before him and said: 'I tell you Norway, I sent that ITP thing back to [the Air Ministry] and I told them they could put it where the monkeys put the nuts!'.

Nevil Shute wondered, 'how many managing directors must have echoed the thought in those days and, unlike Lord Nuffield, had to swallow their principles with their pride'.[16]

For the trouble that Lord Nuffield had caused Airspeed, Nevil Shute felt that he was genuinely sorry and was anxious to help them. Although Lord Nuffield was willing to consider any proposal that Airspeed made to take over the manufacture of Wolseley's aero engines, they had never made a profit and were unable to raise the necessary finance. Airspeed also realised that the manufacture of aero engines was too big for them so, to Nevil Shute's great regret, they let the opportunity go. Nevil Shute blamed the demise of Wolseley aero engines 'fairly and squarely on the Air Ministry's high civil servants of that day, for all their decorations and their knighthoods'. He continued, 'they should have had the wit to handle the business of the country better than that'.[17]

Despite Wolseley's failure to supply aero engines, Airspeed received an ITP from the Air Ministry during October 1936 for the manufacture of 136 twin-engined Oxford trainers, fitted with Armstrong Siddeley Cheetah engines. The 5s preference shares that Airspeed had issued to the public had never been below par until the order for the Oxfords had been received. The shares then started to fall until they had dropped to 1s 6d as investors realised that, owing to the conditions of the ITP, the company's potential 'margin of profit was so small that there would be little hope of reimbursing shareholders for previous losses'.[18] However, after deliveries of the Oxford had started in December 1937, the value of Airspeed's shares began to recover 'as the initial absurdities of the ITP procedure were negotiated out' but Nevil Shute thought that they never 'recovered much above par value'.[19]

The Ministry ordered a further 192 Oxfords during 1937 and 1938 and this aircraft type, which became the standard twin-engine trainer for the British Commonwealth during the Second World War, kept Airspeed operating 'to the limits of its production capacity for the next eight years'.[20] Nevertheless, Nevil Shute commented:

> From this production there was not even the incentive of profit, for essentially the ITP system boiled down to work upon a cost-plus basis with a small margin of profit on whatever the costs happened to be. Ahead of the managing director of Airspeed Ltd. stretched an unknown number of years to be spent in restraining men from spending too much time in the lavatories in order that aeroplanes might cost the taxpayer less, with the reflection that every hour so saved reduced the profit ultimately payable to the company. In time of war the sense of national effort will galvanise a system of that sort, and does so; in time of peace it tends to make a managing director bloody-minded. I think it did with me.[21]

An Airspeed Oxford A.S.10., fitted with Armstrong Siddeley Cheetah engines. (*Flight*)

During January 1937, Wolseley agreed to sell the machinery to manufacture its aero engines to The Scottish Aircraft & Engineering Co. Ltd,[22] for their offshoot the Clyde Aero Engine Co. Ltd, and gave an undertaking to clear the factory within three months. The prospective buyers announced that they hoped to have a factory ready on the Clyde within six months to produce the Wolseley range of aero engines and that these engines would be called Clyde aero-motors.[23] However, the financial accounts for Wolseley Aero Engines Ltd do not show any transaction to suggest that The Scottish Aircraft & Engineering Co. Ltd actually bought any machinery from Wolseley. This would, in fact, appear to be the case as on 2 June 1937, *The Aeroplane* reported that:

> …the machine-tools are still where they were in the Wolseley works and could be started up at any time. Doing so would be wise. The Scorpio was, or rather is, the only motor of its particular size and type. And it definitely fills a place in the needs of the British Aircraft Industry. The Scorpio, particularly, fitted the Airspeed Envoy, and no doubt other aircraft constructors who are considering producing an aeroplane in that particular category would be glad of the Scorpio.

Eight weeks after the appearance of *The Aeroplane*'s comments, on 26 July 1937, The Scottish Aircraft and Engineering Co. Ltd went into receivership with what appears to have been a total loss to shareholders[24] and, despite the potential, Clyde Aero Engine's planned venture did not materialise. This prompted *The Aeroplane* to publish the following, on 23 February 1938, under the heading 'What a Pity':

> Most readers of this paper know that Wolseley Aero Engines Ltd., had produced an extraordinarily good motor called the Scorpio just when Lord Nuffield became fed up with the Air Ministry and decided to shut down, after having spent approximately half a million pounds on laying out a first class factory and producing the first batch of first class motors.
>
> There has seldom been a better example of the unhappy results which can follow the sudden impulses of a very rich man. The Scorpio engine happened to be of a size which does not exist in this country but does exist in the United States, and it would just have filled the gap for certain sizes of Service machines and for private aeroplanes which, if properly cultivated in a businesslike way, would have soon paid back Lord Nuffield's money.
>
> But although the Scorpio was pretty well known, few people ever knew that the Wolseley Aries motor had got past the test-bench stage. And we doubt whether anybody except Airspeed Ltd. ever knew that there were any Aries motors in use. Therefore there is the more interest in the following letter to W.S. Shackleton Ltd.

Ansett Airways Airspeed Envoy VH-UXM seen over Melbourne, *c*.1938. This machine was previously registered G-ACVI and named *Miss Wolseley*.

This advertisement appeared around 1937.

'Dear Sirs,- We have pleasure in giving you the following details of a very successful run recently completed by one of our Wolseley 'Aries' Mk III engines using Shell Aviation Gasoline (77 octane) and Aero Shell Medium Oil.

This engine, no. 17, was installed in our Airspeed Envoy on 16th June 1937, and was taken out for overhaul on 22nd October 1937, having then done 596 hours. During this time the engine had required little more than the usual servicing and throughout gave complete satisfaction. The oil was not changed, whilst the consumption settled down after the first few hours to 3 to 4 pints per hour.

Inspection after dismantling showed all the parts to be in very good order – as is usual with this oil, there was positively no sign of sludge - the piston rings were free in the grooves, the oil drain-holes in the scraper-rings and ring-grooves were merely as though thinly lacquered black – this latter also applies to the interior of all pistons. Reduction gear and rear section crankcase components were as though wetted with clean oil.

> *This experience further confirms the opinion long held by the writer, that use of the correct grade of Aero Shell is a guarantee against lubrication trouble.*
> *Yours Faithfully, Ansett Airways Limited.*
> *(Signed) J.J. Davies, Chief Engineer.'*

Even allowing for the fact that everybody knows that 'that's Shell that was,' and 'the times change though Shell does not,' except from season to season of course, this letter shows that an unusually good motor, which might have done much to increase the reputation of British aircraft was brought to an untimely end.

Although the manufacturing operations of Wolseley Aero Engines Ltd were closed in August 1936, the company remained in existence and for the twelve months ending 31 August 1937, it recorded a loss of £12,550 2s 10d (about half a million at 2006 values). However, if the company had not sold seven aero engines from stock during this period, this loss would have exceeded £19,000. Wolseley's efforts to enter the aero engine manufacturing business finally came to an end in September 1937, when Wolseley Aero Engines Ltd was merged with Nuffield Mechanizations Ltd, to form Nuffield Mechanizations & Aero Ltd, a company that made tanks, tank engines, Bren Gun carriers, Bofors anti-aircraft guns and many other munitions during the Second World War.

Notes

1 Flt-Lt Colman, a retired RAF trained officer, was employed by Airspeed Ltd as a test pilot for a salary of £400 per annum, about £19,000 at 2006 values. Sadly, he was killed over Northern France in 1941, while flying a Bristol Beaufighter.
2 Shute, Nevil, p.209.
3 Shute, Nevil, p.191.
4 Lewis, Peter, p.285.
5 Shute, Nevil, p.234.
6 With Wolseley Aries engines, a price of £4,800 was quoted. See Middleton, D.H., p.90.
7 CMD 5295, p.6.
8 Ibid.
9 Ibid.
10 Ibid.
11 CMD 5295, p.7.
12 When William Cannell became redundant as a result of the closure of Wolseley's aero engine business, he received £10,000, about half a million at 2006 values, as compensation from Lord Nuffield, paid out of Lord Nuffield's own funds.
13 *The Aeroplane*, 14 October 1936.
14 Shute, Nevil, pp.235, 236.
15 Ibid.
16 Shute, Nevil, p.237.
17 Shute, Nevil, pp.237, 238.
18 Shute, Nevil, p.244.
19 Shute, Nevil, p.245.
20 Shute, Nevil, p.243.
21 Ibid.
22 The Scottish Aircraft and Engineering Co. Ltd. had been formed in June 1936 to acquire a licence to develop and build the American-designed Burnelli 'flying-wing' airliner in Britain. See Orde-Hume, W.J.G., p.147.
23 *The Aeroplane*, 27 January 1937, p.88.
24 Ord-Hume, W.J.G., p.147.

7

LORD NUFFIELD'S CONTROVERSY BECOMES PUBLIC

In a speech given in London during the middle of October 1936, the Minister of Health, Sir Kingsley Wood, praised Lord Nuffield for his gift of £1.25 million to Oxford University for the establishment of a post-graduate medical school. The Minister said that 'it was impossible to over-estimate all that it would mean. It would be of tremendous aid to research activities, and might have a vital bearing on the health of the nation. The potentialities of a post-graduate school, such as the one now made possible at Oxford, were enormous'. Details of the donation, which was said to be the largest single gift made by an individual donor to any British university, were given in the national Press, thereby heightening Lord Nuffield's popularity and his reputation as a generous benefactor.[1]

A few days later, on 22 October 1936, Lord Nuffield delivered a statement to representatives of the Press, whom he had invited to hear it. He:

> ...traced the history of his communications with the Air Ministry on the subject of the manufacture of Wolseley aero-engines and parts, and of his decision to close the Wolseley Aero Engine works and not to allow Wolseley Motors, Limited, to take a share in the shadow industry for the making of aero-engine parts to be assembled at a central factory.[2]

Lord Nuffield issued copies of correspondence exchanged between himself and the Air Ministry and declared that he regretted the situation keenly, but statements by the Air Ministry had left him with no option but to put forward his side. He emphasised that no question of percentage profit, costing methods, or any other financial aspect was ever raised, although this had been a suggestion as a reason for his action in withdrawing from the Shadow industry. He also wanted to scotch malicious rumours concerning his lack of co-operation with other motor industry magnates.

Lord Nuffield explained that he had set up Wolseley's aero engine factory in 1929, financing it with his own money, and continued, 'Throughout the whole development period [of Wolseley's aero engines] there had been a complete lack of support from the political interests at the Air Ministry, although help had been freely given by the technical side'.[3] He said that headway had been slow, in spite of this help, and five years passed before the Air Ministry would accept a Wolseley aero engine for trial, even though the type had passed the regulation tests under Air Ministry supervision in the factory.

Lord Nuffield said that in July 1935, he had written to Lord Swinton, the Air Minister, asking if he might call on him on a certain day to seek his advice – but he was told that an appointment for that day could not possibly be given.[4] He drew attention to the fact that there was no suggestion of an alternative date and that there was no indication his co-operation was desired.

'That,' said Lord Nuffield, 'was the first time in my life I had been turned down by a Cabinet Minister'.[5]

Turning to the subject of the Shadow Factory scheme, Lord Nuffield emphasised that he had been against the scheme from the beginning. He believed delays would arise from unpunctual deliveries and a bomb dropped on one of the Shadow Factories would upset production as a whole.

> As a practical engineer, [Lord Nuffield] thought that in any undertaking of such technical precision, as the construction of aero-engines, unity of control was essential; and he could not visualise the Shadow scheme developing with the necessary efficiency and speed. This, he said, was [just] one of his reasons for not coming in. But his main reason was that he already had an aero-motor factory which the Ministry refused to recognise, apparently because they deemed it unsuitable or unlikely to be efficiently operated.[6]

Lord Nuffield was of the opinion that 'The whole matter is simply a difference of opinion on the principles of production' and said that 'as the largest manufacturer of internal combustion engines in this country, I can claim some experience in this connection.'[7] Anxious to help, he offered to build 2,000 Bristol aero engines in Wolseley's aero engine factory at the price the Air Ministry was already paying, but that offer was turned down even though he had promised to start deliveries of these engines in approximately six months.

Lord Nuffield believed that the Air Ministry had deliberately neglected his aero engine production facilities and, in conclusion, said 'his executives and technicians had got on quite well with the technical and engineering sides of the Air Ministry, just as they had with the War Office, but with the political side of the Air Ministry he found himself at variance'.[8] In reply to a question, Lord Nuffield said that, 'the [aero engine] factory was still there with a skeleton staff and that if he were wanted he was always ready to help'.[9]

Now out in the open, the controversy brought to light another offer to make aero engines which had also been turned down by the Air Ministry. On 23 October 1936, the day after Lord Nuffield's meeting with the Press, T.G. John, the chairman and managing director of the Alvis Car & Engineering Co. Ltd, issued the following announcement:[10]

> Since Lord Nuffield made his public statement with regard to his dispute with the Air Ministry the name of my company has, unfortunately, been used through no desire or action on our part. These circumstances caused me to state the position so far as my company is concerned. We have no quarrel with the Air Ministry and we are on most friendly terms with all concerned.
>
> My company came into the aero-engine industry in the early part of last year [1935], some months before there was any talk of the necessity of rapid expansion of our air force. This was done after full consideration, and in the belief that there would be good commercial markets both at home and abroad for our engines. The technical position was surveyed and arrangements were made to manufacture an aero-engine of high international reputation which we believed to have merits at least equal to, and probably greater than, any other.
>
> Before making production arrangements, I consulted the Air Ministry. I was informed that whilst they would help us technically as much as they could, there was no possibility of our receiving orders from them. Naturally, I protested, and in later correspondence set out my reasons in detail why the official policy was not, in my opinion, in the best national interests. Notwithstanding this, we proceeded with the completion of our aero-engine factory, in which we installed the most modern plant and equipment for the manufacture of our aero-engines, with full confidence that there would be a ready market for them.

T.G. John, managing
director of the Alvis
Car & Engineering Co.

From time to time we informed the Air Ministry of the progress we were making. Our first knowledge of the shadow factory scheme was gleaned from newspapers some six months ago. I immediately spoke to the Director of Aircraft Production, pointing out that I could not understand why new factories were to be built at public expense while our own very large and modern factory, built and equipped by us especially for making large sized aero-engines, was being ignored officially. At his suggestion, I wrote to Lord Weir asking for an appointment to discuss the matter, and Lord Weir replied immediately by telegram.

I was courteously received and for two hours Lord Weir discussed the whole position with me. I was amazed to learn however, until my visit he had no knowledge of the fact that we had a large, modern air-engine factory which was then ready for production. He invited my free criticism of his shadow factory scheme, and argued his views with considerable ability. I did not agree with him on many points, particularly on the expected efficiency of the shadow factories, but I had no doubt whatsoever of his honesty of purpose. As far as Alvis was concerned, Lord Weir assured me that our resources were of considerable national value and would be considered in this respect. This conversation was confirmed by me in a letter a few days later. Unfortunately, this letter was never acknowledged, and we have heard nothing since.

Although the Air Ministry have not yet taken advantage of our resources, we are so confident that military and civil conditions both at home and abroad in the immediate future will demand a rapidly growing supply of aero-engines of this type to meet requirements that we have proceeded with our plans, and during the next few weeks the first aero-engines out of this factory will be on test. Rapid production will follow.

In saying all this, I realize that the Air Ministry have a difficult problem to face. For many years after the [First World] War its activities were drastically curtailed while other nations continued to maintain and expand their own air forces. Cabinets were faced with peace and League of Nations propaganda and disarmament conferences that ended abortively. The Air Ministry was but a skeleton department. It was under-staffed and subject to all sorts of restrictions imposed by the Treasury, hindered and hampered by Parliamentary opposition, and its work slowed up by well-intentioned plans for reorganised defence measures.

Every one wants to help the Air Ministry to obtain the biggest number of aeroplanes possible, but at the same time they must be better than those of any other country in quality and performance, and I think that all efforts, nationally and individually, must be directed to this end.

Being well known and much respected, Lord Nuffield's statement to the Press was widely reported and it sparked off a wave of criticism about the Government's rearmament programme. Five days after Lord Nuffield's statement, on 28 October 1936, the Government responded by issuing a White Paper (CMD 5295), which was drafted by the Air Ministry under Lord Swinton's direction, setting out the Shadow Factory scheme and giving their account of the controversy but the Air Ministry, and Swinton himself, could not escape the censure.

In his book, W.J. Reader[11] maintains that:

The main fault to be found with the White Paper, in the light of what we know now, is that it makes rather too much of the Air Ministry's inability to guarantee a market for aero-engines, and exaggerates the aircraft makers' freedom to choose what engines they would buy. This was no doubt in theory perfectly true, but from what we have seen of the power which the Ministry was increasingly exercising, it was a slightly dishonest argument to use.

He goes on to say, '...the Ministry was too set in its ways; too much inclined to keep aero engine business within a tight comfortable ring; too ready to accept the ring's optimistic accounts of its own productive capacity'.

On 29 October, 1936, Lord Nuffield's dispute with the Air Ministry was debated[12] in the House of Lords and in response to a question from Lord Snell, who asked 'whether His Majesty's Government would make a statement regarding the organisation of the production of aero engines for the Royal Air Force', Lord Swinton said:

I am obliged to the noble lord for the opportunity of making a short statement on this matter. The White Paper which has been issued sets out very fully the facts both as to the policy of His Majesty's Government and also as to the discussions which have taken place with my noble friend Lord Nuffield and his representatives. It will be seen from the White Paper that His Majesty's Government have decided to adopt a policy with which my noble friend is unfortunately not in agreement, and I regret very much that that should be the case.

His Majesty's Government have, however, made their decision upon the considered advice of the experienced firms which are undertaking the work of constructing the engines that are required, and we believe it will prove successful. I have nothing to add to the White Paper except that I wish to say that I regret sincerely that my noble friend should feel that I treated him with any lack of consideration. I was greatly pressed at the time he asked to see me and I hope he will believe that the last thing in the world I intended was to be discourteous to him.

I have Lord Nuffield's authority for saying that, while he cannot agree with some of the opinions expressed, he accepts the White Paper as a fair statement of the Government's point of view and of what passed between himself and the Air Ministry: and that he does not propose to make any further statement on the subject of his part in the discussions. Although he is not able to co-operate in the air-engine plan, he holds himself ready to place his services at the disposal of the Government for other important work. (Cheers).

The Labour peer, Lord Strabolgi,[13] said:

> that his colleagues on the Opposition side were very satisfied with the last a part of the Secretary of State's reply… As to the question of aero-engines, he wished to say at once that from the study he made of the White Paper and of the statements made elsewhere by Lord Nuffield and the managing director of the Alvis Company, Lord Swinton, and all the other parties concerned, appeared to have acted in the national interest according to their lights in the present circumstances. He did not lend himself to any of the rather florid attacks made in certain quarters on one side or the other.

Lord Strabolgi thought it was a little unfortunate that Lord Swinton should have felt himself bound to reply to a request for an interview by Lord Nuffield in the way he did.

> If the Labour Party was in power and Lord Ponsonby was the First Lord of the Admiralty – [laughter] – and he refused to see him on some matter affecting naval construction, he would be hurt as well as surprised. They were bound to take note of the fact that similar trouble had arisen in the past and would rise again for the same reasons, and that it led to accusations of the formation of rings – which he did not support… Did he understand that the factory erected by Lord Nuffield at a cost of £500,000 was not going to be used at the present juncture for supplying aeroplane engines?

Continuing, Lord Strabolgi said that he understood that the factory was going to be used for the War Office and not for aeroplane engines to which Lord Nuffield, who was occupying a seat on the Government side of the house, nodded assent and said that it was going to be used for making engines for army tanks.[14]

Later in the debate, Lord Sempill[15] said that:

> …their lordships would deplore the fact that it became necessary for one of this country's greatest industrialists to come forward and defend himself against an issue brought to public notice by the Government Department concerned. At a time when the affairs of Europe were in the melting-pot, and when we should obviously be standing squarely together prepared to meet any emergency, publicity of this nature could not have come at a more unfortunate moment. The fact that the matter had come to a head at this juncture was to be deplored. It raised an issue of the most far-reaching importance, and, however amicably the present situation might be resolved, grave misgivings must remain in their lordships' minds. The fact that the country should have lost, from an aircraft point of view, Lord Nuffield's great organising and manufacturing ability and single minded desire to help his country was regrettable in the extreme, and appeared to be the result of the policy which had clogged the efficiency of our aircraft design and production system for many years past.
>
> The Air Minister had inherited a system which had long proved an anachronism. The Air Ministry divided firms into two categories – approved and disapproved. The approved list was selected as far back as 1920, and was limited to a total of four engine and 18 aeroplane manufacturers, which had since been reduced by retirements and amalgamation. Had the Air Ministry encouraged the young and enterprising, new and unapproved firms – 16 in number, representing a capital outlay of nearly £5,000,000 – who had proved themselves successful in designing and producing civil aircraft and engines, and had given them equal advantages with the selected firms, the competitive element would have produced in this country a field of choice equal, if not superior, to anything elsewhere.

The hazardous procedure adopted by the Air Ministry in its expansion programme must inevitably depend for its success on the building up of production based on machines which had not been thoroughly tried out. The present situation was without parallel in this country. They saw in existence an armament ring which, though it might have had some justification in 1920, was not capable of coping with the expansion necessary now. The Government had cast away the substance for the shadow. The shadow programme at the present moment was one of bricks and mortar. Without the experience of administration, economic management, supervisory capacity and technical ability, a scheme of quantitative production could not be carried out efficiently. Let them not be misled. They had arrived at a point where old methods must give way to new requirements. They must call on all available resources and not rely only on a few selected firms.

Their lordships must satisfy themselves that all sides of aircraft production were developed in the most efficient way. It was not sufficient to produce good engines if the air frame and equipment were not of equal standard.. The present situation would be even worse had it not been that a member of their lordships' House had recently given to it his undivided attention.[16]

On the same day, 29 October 1936, the dispute between Lord Nuffield and the Air Ministry was also debated in the House of Commons and, after the Leader of the Opposition, Mr Attlee, requested a statement regarding the Government's air programme, Sir Philip Sassoon, the Under-Secretary for Air, reiterated a similar account to that given by Lord Swinton in the House of Lords. However, there was laughter from the Opposition and cries of 'Oh!' when he said that Lord Swinton had not intended to be discourteous to Lord Nuffield.

The Times, in their leader on 29 October 1936, commented on the cause of the controversy as follows:

> There is little reason to doubt that the personal issue arose from a clash of temperaments which might never have reached the stage of public revelation if there had been a little less impetuosity on one side and a little more tact on the other.

If Lord Nuffield was seen to be impetuous he was no doubt displaying an anxiety to provide some work for his aero engine factory in order to get a return on the vast amount of money he had invested into the business regardless of profit while, at the same time, highlighting a need to prepare the country for war. Accordingly, Lord Nuffield must have been very pleased when he gained support in his disagreement with the Air Ministry from Winston Churchill who, seeing an opportunity to make an attack on the Government's rearmament programme, said, on 12 November 1936, during a defence debate, 'The revelations for which Lord Nuffield was responsible were important because, like a lightning flash, they had revealed a dark and confused landscape of Air and Army production'. Churchill demanded a Parliamentary inquiry as the Government was falling behind in the programme to complete 1,500 aircraft by March 1937, and, said Lord Weir:

> …held a very anomalous position. He has neither formal authority nor official responsibility. If there are misgivings, they can be dismissed with the assurance that Lord Weir has the matter in his hands. If things go wrong Lord Weir can justly answer that he is not responsible, but is only working in an advisory capacity. Neither the functions of the Minister for the Co-ordination of Defence nor those entrusted to Lord Weir are compatible with any sound system of organisation.[17]

Soon after the dispute with Lord Nuffield, Lord Weir and the Air Ministry became embroiled in another conflict, this time with the Admiralty who wished to regain control of the Fleet Air Arm. A critical report into civil aviation added to Swinton's difficulties but, as he sat in the House of Lords, he was unable to reply to his critics in the House of Commons face to face. Although the Prime Minister, Neville Chamberlain, defended Swinton on several occasions, he subsequently decided his Air Minister must sit in the House of Commons – so Swinton was obliged to resign on 12 May 1938. On hearing of Lord Swinton's dismissal, Lord Weir also resigned.

Despite the setbacks involved in the manufacture of aero engines, both Lord Nuffield and his Organization continued their involvement in aviation, as outlined in the next chapters and in Appendix 1.

Notes

1   Lord Nuffield's offer of a donation was contained in a letter addressed to the vice-chancellor of Oxford University on 10 October 1936 (Lord Nuffield's fifty-ninth birthday), the text of which, together with the vice-chancellor's reply, appears in *The Times*, 16 October 1936. Lord Nuffield later increased his donation to £2 million, about £88 million at 2006 values.

2   *The Times*, 23 October 1936.

3   Ibid.

4   The text of Lord Nuffield's letter and Lord Swinton's reply appears on page 79.

5   *The Times*, 23 October 1936.

6   *The Aeroplane*, 28 October 1936, p.526.

7   Ibid.

8   *The Aeroplane*, 28 October 1936, p.527.

9   Ibid.

10 As reported in *The Times*, 26 October 1936.

11 Reader, W.J., pp.266, 268.

12 As reported in *The Times*, Friday 30 October 1936.

13 As Lt-Cdr J.M. Kenworthy, Lord Strabolgi (1886–1953), whose title went back to the fourteenth century, served in the First World War as a naval commander. He was one of the early MPs of the Labour movement, elected in 1926 after having served in Parliament as a Liberal.

14 As reported in *The Times*, Friday 30 October 1936.

15 William Frances Forbes-Sempill/Lord Sempill was an engineer, author, aviator and sometime the president of The Royal Aeronautical Society. His profile appears on pp.181–182.

16 As reported in *The Times*, Friday 30 October 1936.

17 Reader, W.J., pp.268, 269.

8

THE HESTON TYPE 5 AIRCRAFT

At the beginning of 1938, Lord Nuffield became interested in another aspect of aviation when he had a discussion with Major F.B. Halford, the technical director of D. Napier & Sons. Being an ardent patriot, Lord Nuffield agreed to donate £16,678 (about £690,000 at 2006 values) so that two Heston Type 5 high-speed monoplanes could be built for the dual purpose of gaining air speed records for Britain and acting as test beds for the new Napier-Halford Sabre engine, which was destined to power the Hawker Typhoon and Tempest fighter aircraft.

The Heston Type 5 aircraft was designed to have a flight duration of eighteen minutes and be capable of 480mph but, due to the outbreak of war and teething troubles with the complex and powerful twenty-four-cylinder 'H' type, 2,300hp, sleeve valve, Sabre engine, the first of the two aircraft did not complete its taxiing trials until the spring of 1940. Although the war had put an end to civilian flying, and thereby any thought of contending speed records, an appeal was made to the Air Ministry for permission to evaluate the aircraft in the hope that it might be found to have a wartime application. Approval having been granted, the aircraft – G-AFOK – took off for its maiden flight on 12 June 1940, but its pilot, Sqn Ldr G.L.G. Richmond, quickly decided to return to the airfield as not only was the Sabre engine overheating but the machine was also proving difficult to control. Fortunately, Sqn Ldr Richmond was unhurt when the aircraft stalled on finals and crash landed after only seven minutes of flight, causing severe damage to its wooden construction. Although the second aircraft – G-AFOL – was at an advanced stage of construction, at that time it was decided to abandon the project because other priorities were being created by the war.

The construction of this Heston Type 5 aircraft, for the dual purposes of gaining air-speed records for Britain and acting as a test bed for the Napier-Halford Sabre engine, was financed by Lord Nuffield.

9

THE CASTLE BROMWICH
AIRCRAFT FACTORY

On 20 May 1938, a few days after Lord Swinton's departure, the new Air Minister, Sir Kingsley Wood, made peace with Lord Nuffield by inviting him to lunch at 10 Downing Street. (During his previous appointment as Minister of Health, Sir Kingsley Wood had praised Lord Nuffield about his donation to Oxford University for the establishment of a post-graduate medical school, see page 113). According to Major Bulman of the Air Ministry, Sir Kingsley Wood 'was a kindly man [and] vastly more approachable than his predecessor'.[1] The Minister asked Lord Nuffield to enter aircraft production by constructing and running a factory on behalf of the Air Ministry for the mass production of Vickers Supermarine Spitfires, using semi-skilled labour. Lord Nuffield agreed on the 'understanding that there should be a minimum amount of interference ... from the Air Ministry to enable the position to be tackled in a somewhat different way to the present Shadow [Factory] Scheme ...'[2] He also insisted that neither he, as controller, nor Oliver Boden, his deputy controller, should receive any remuneration from the Air Ministry, as he regarded the appointments to be of national service.

The Government wanted the factory to be built in Liverpool as it was an area with high unemployment but, although he appreciated the human problem in the Liverpool area, Lord Nuffield pointed out that the time needed to train large numbers of unskilled labour would delay the production of Spitfires so the choice of location for the new factory was then left to Lord Nuffield and Oliver Boden. They decided that the factory should be built on a 345-acre site at Castle Bromwich, Birmingham, due to the availability of suitable labour in that area and because the smoky atmosphere, which was prevalent in the city at that time, gave some natural protection against aerial attack.

Construction of the factory, which had 52.5 acres of buildings (now part of Jaguar Cars Ltd), started on 1 July 1938, when Sir Kingsley Wood cut the first sod and although aircraft production had got underway in some departments by August 1939, building work continued until the summer of 1940. The original plan was for the factory to manufacture sixty Spitfires per week, but it was then decided that heavy bombers should also be made at the plant and that the output of Spitfires should be halved.

However, difficulties were encountered while the production facilities to manufacture Spitfires were being set up at the Castle Bromwich factory for several reasons.

> ...First the drawings were late; further the drawings themselves were designed for a different process of manufacture and, as was appropriate to craftsman production, not all of them were fully dimensioned. Numerous alterations of the drawings had to be made, and final modifications were not possible in some details until there had been trial assembly of the

Above: Sir Kingsley Wood, Air Minister (left), in discussion with Lord Nuffield (right), at Castle Bromwich Aircraft Factory on 1 July 1938. Oliver Boden (centre) is looking on.

Right: Lord Nuffield enjoying a joke with Sir Kingsley Wood, who is seen cutting the first sod for the foundations of Castle Bromwich Aircraft Factory, Birmingham, on 1 July 1938.

finished component and the component itself had been assembled into the first aircraft, after which, of course, the necessary modifications had to be made to tools. The changes in production schedule to include bombers were also responsible for some delays. It took some time for the authorities to decide precisely what bomber was to be produced in the factory, and at various dates, plans were made for the production of particular class of bomber, only to be discarded in favour of construction of some other type. Further, with the imminence and advent of war, production at Supermarine factories took priority, since at any one time they had a number of aircraft awaiting completion, and the sending of parts from Castle Bromwich enabled a more rapid increase in immediate output. While Castle Bromwich was completing its organisation, such a diversion of parts led to no difficulty, but the case was different when they approached the end of this preliminary period and could look forward to seeing their own planes being assembled.[3]

Difficulties were also experienced in introducing the system for the mass production of Spitfires as frequent design changes, to improve the fighter's performance, often called for alterations to be made to the jigs and tools used in this type of manufacture. In addition, 'the huge amount of curvature on the design of the [Spitfire's] wings, tail unit and fuselage made both the manufacture of panels and assembly a nightmare'.[4] All this, together with the enormous task of training a semi-skilled workforce inside unfinished buildings, meant that there was a considerable delay in completing the first aircraft at the Castle Bromwich factory.

A further setback occurred on 6 March 1940 when Oliver Boden died suddenly at the age of fifty-three while on his way to London to attend a conference.

Oliver Boden had been a most able production engineer who had started his career at Vickers during the First World War where he had organised the manufacture of armaments. When Lord Nuffield purchased Wolseley Motors Ltd in 1927, Boden was the works manager of the company and at the time of his death he was Lord Nuffield's deputy and managing director of both Morris Motors Ltd and Nuffield Mechanizations & Aero Ltd in addition to his responsibilities at the Castle Bromwich factory. According to Miles Thomas, his typical daily schedule to cope with his heavy workload had been to rise at 7 a.m., at his home in Warmley to the north-east of Birmingham, then:

> …take a scanty breakfast and be driven to the Castle Bromwich Spitfire Factory, then on to the Tank Factory on the Wolseley grounds. He would have discussions with departmental heads and then be driven to Cowley, where he would again have meetings and handle correspondence. From Oxford, he went by train to London, talked to officials at the Ministry or War Office, where he was much respected; caught an afternoon train back to Oxford, spent some time in his office, and then was driven back to Warmley, reaching home between 8 and 9 p.m. for a late evening meal'[5]

Lord Nuffield said of Oliver Boden:

> He has been described in an obituary notice as my right-hand man, and no cognomen could be more appropriate… the services he rendered me constantly increased in worth and importance…. His entire distaste for any form of self publicity has resulted in his name being less widely known than would otherwise be the case, but those who were near to him were automatically made aware of his engineering and commercial genius, complimented by instincts so generous as to gain him affection in no less measure than admiration…[6]

After his death, Oliver Boden's position as deputy controller of the Castle Bromwich factory was taken by his assistant, Herbert Clark.

Supermarine Spitfires, Mark LF XVIe, under construction at the Castle Bromwich Aircraft Factory during the spring of 1945. This factory is presently occupied by Jaguar Cars Ltd. (Jaguar Daimler Heritage Trust)

As a result of the escalating crisis during the period before Dunkirk, in the spring of 1940:

> the decision was taken that maximum output of Spitfires over [a period of] six weeks was to override any other considerations. The completion of semi-finished planes at the Supermarine works accordingly ranked above the production schedule of Castle Bromwich; its management accepted this position, and were accordingly prepared to give the Vickers organisation whatever parts they wanted.[7]

At a time of national emergency when two separate, but collaborating, organisations were under extreme pressure to make Spitfires, one trying desperately to get the aircraft into mass production and the other striving to increase its production, it is not surprising a conflict arose between them. Such a conflict occurred when the management at Castle Bromwich asked representatives of Vickers, who appeared to assume they had the right to walk into the Castle Bromwich works and take what they liked, to submit lists of their needs before visiting the factory in order to prevent the production process from being disrupted. (Herbert Clark later reported that the Castle Bromwich factory had supplied some 386,000 parts and a quantity of main planes to Vickers Supermarine's factories and to Service.) Quoting from *The Life of Lord Nuffield*:[8]

> ...it seems clear the Vickers management was told that Castle Bromwich was being unco-operative and reported accordingly to the Minister of Aircraft Production. It also seems probable that the overriding need for fighter aircraft had led to a natural irritation in the Air Ministry itself that more Spitfires were not available, and this was readily concentrated on the large new factory which had not so far produced a complete plane.[9]

On 17 May 1940 the situation came to a head when the Minister, Lord Beaverbrook, decided that Vickers should take over the factory and operate it alongside their own. Lord Nuffield, then aged sixty-three, was shocked by the Minister's lack of prior consultation and by the abruptness of the decision, which he received by telephone. This is not surprising, when considering the amount of time and effort that both he and his staff had spent establishing the factory. He vociferously defended his colleagues at Castle Bromwich as he felt 'the Whitehall authorities were not sufficiently aware of the extent they had in fact gone out of their way to supply Vickers'.[10]

In all this, the Castle Bromwich factory was in the tactically weak position as it had not yet come into full production but, three weeks later, on 6 June 1940, the efforts of Lord Nuffield and his staff were seen to bear fruit when the first Castle Bromwich-built Spitfire was delivered to the RAF. By 1 April 1941, a total of 650 Spitfires had left the factory and:

> Vickers were the first to admit that much of the jigging and tooling that Oliver Boden and [Herbert] 'Chicago' Clark had put into Castle Bromwich were extremely effective in increasing the output of Spitfires, once the line had began to roll and the constant stream of modifications had been organised into the production pattern.[11]

Despite all the initial difficulties, 11,939 Spitfires had been produced at Castle Bromwich Aircraft Factory by the end of the war, out of a grand total of 20,443 built, as well as a quantity of Avro Lancaster bombers.

Notes

1 Bulman, G.P., p.258.
2 Andrews and Brunner, p.228.
3 Andrews and Brunner, p.229.
4 Bingham, Victor F., p.17.
5 Thomas, Sir Miles, p.197.
6 *The Autocar*, 15 March 1940, p.280.
7 Andrews and Brunner, p.230.
8 Ibid.
9 Ibid.
10 Ibid.
11 Thomas, Sir Miles, p.205.

FINALE

Lord Nuffield's disagreements with the Air Ministry, during the mid-1930s concerned two entirely separate issues. The first involved Wolseley's proposed entry into the Shadow Factory scheme while the second related to the supply of Wolseley Scorpio engines for fitment into Airspeed Oxford aircraft.

It was unfortunate that Lord Nuffield was visiting Australia in April 1936, when the heads of seven motor firms, including Wolseley's managing director, met the Air Minister to learn of the Shadow Factory scheme for the manufacture of aero engines. Lord Nuffield, seemingly, knew nothing of the scheme until he returned to England at the beginning of May 1936, whereupon he took a disliking to it as he wished to make complete engines rather than sections of them. Also, he probably felt that he had been sidelined as his great rival in the manufacture of motor vehicles, Lord Austin, had been appointed chairman of the Shadow Factory's Aero-Engine Committee. If Lord Nuffield had been more flexible and the Air Ministry had shown more diplomacy, perhaps their subsequent negotiations would have had a positive outcome. Nevertheless, with the benefit of hindsight, there is no doubt that Lord Nuffield should have allowed Wolseley to join the Shadow Factory scheme to manufacture Bristol aero engines as, despite his concerns over its viability, the scheme proved to be successful.

The political correspondent of *The Times* commented on the situation as follows:

> Lord Nuffield's strong independent individualism is well known, and no one doubts his intense patriotism. But the qualities of such a man are not always easily turned to team-work, and the official mind is perhaps not best fitted to handle them.[1]

Wolseley's withdrawal from the Shadow Factory scheme caused a rift between Leonard Lord, the managing director of Morris Motors Ltd, who was in favour of the scheme, and Lord Nuffield. After Leonard Lord resigned, apparently due to his association with a female staff member at the Cowley factory, the pair later became rivals when Lord joined the Austin Motor Co. With Lord Nuffield's money and Leonard Lord's skills as a production engineer, they were a formidable team. If Leonard Lord had remained with Morris Motors Ltd, it is doubtful whether the company would have merged with the Austin Motor Co. in 1952 to form the British Motor Corporation. This being the case, both Morris Motors Ltd and the Austin Motor Co. would have taken an entirely different course after the Second World War.

Lord Nuffield's decision to end his foray into the manufacture of aero engines in 1936, following his aversion to the terms contained in an Air Ministry's contract for the supply of 300 Wolseley Scorpios, resulted in one of his rare business failures. Without the need to worry about shareholders' opinions, as he owned Wolseley Aero Engines Ltd himself, and because he had no fear of financial disaster, Lord Nuffield was able to adopt a robust line in his dealings with the Air Ministry and dictate his position. Although he suffered a substantial financial loss, this loss did not have a detrimental effect on the rest of Lord Nuffield's business, owing to his immense personal wealth, but Britain lost a fledgling aero engine manufacturer at a time when Germany was re-arming and war looked inevitable.

In his own sphere, that of a motor manufacturer, Lord Nuffield was supreme and the saga of Wolseley Aero Engines Ltd remains a byway in the life of one of Britain's most successful industrialists.

Notes

1   *The Times*, Saturday 24 October 1936.

APPENDICES

APPENDIX 1

A) THE NUFFIELD ORGANIZATION'S INVOLVEMENT WITH AVIATION DURING THE SECOND WORLD WAR

On the outbreak of the Second World War, the Nuffield Organization, which was then the largest manufacturer of cars and commercial vehicles in Britain, had twelve factories and a workforce of 20,000. By the time the war had ended, even though much of its workforce had been 'called up for the duration', the number of the Organization's employees had increased to 30,000 and it was operating sixty-three factories.

When war was declared in September 1939, Lord Nuffield turned his factories over to making aircraft and aircraft components in addition to manufacturing military vehicles, tanks, Bren Gun carriers, Bofors anti-aircraft guns, torpedoes, mines, mine sinkers, and many other products to support the war effort.

1) Morris Motors Ltd, Cowley, Oxford

On 22 May 1939 Morris Motors Ltd became the first vehicle manufacturer in Britain to make 1,000,000 vehicles. Four months later, in September 1939, Lord Nuffield accepted an invitation from the Air Minister, Sir Kingsley Wood, to take control of the repair of damaged aircraft for the RAF, and he joined the Air Ministry as Director-General of Maintenance. Within a short time the headquarters of the Civilian Repair Organization (CRO) had been set up as a new unit of the RAF under the civilian control at Morris Motors Ltd Cowley. The Air Ministry insisted that companies who were engaged in the manufacture of aircraft should be not be distracted from their task so, to enable the CRO to be expanded, Lord Nuffield made use of businesses which were involved with civil aviation. He also made use of motor vehicle distributors whose showrooms and workshops were under utilised due to the war, and five main CRO repair depots were soon established. These were served, eventually, by a network of some 1,500 Civilian Repair Units (CRUs).

In November 1939, an initial batch of damaged Spitfires and Hurricanes arrived for repair at the No.1 CRU, which was located within Morris Motors' factory at Cowley. As the number suggests, this was the first CRU to be set up and by the time of the evacuation from Dunkirk, during May/June 1940, it had a staff of 800 who were repairing, on average, twelve machines

An example of a trailer-mounted 40mm Bofors anti-aircraft gun made by Nuffield Mechanizations & Aero Ltd at their factory in Gosford Street, Coventry, during the Second World War. The first batch of Nuffield-made Bofors guns was delivered to the Army in June 1939, after which output from the Gosford Street factory rose from five to fifty a week.

Above: An aerial view of the Morris Motors' factory at Cowley, c.1937.

Opposite page: Three views of the Civilian Repair Unit at the Morris Motors' factory, Cowley. This unit repaired over 80,000 aircraft during the Second World War and returned them to the RAF to fight another day.

Top: Hawker Hurricanes undoing repair. (British Motor Industry Heritage Trust)

Middle: Lord Nuffield using a micrometer to measure a component. A Hawker Hurricane can be seen in the background. (British Motor Industry Heritage Trust)

Bottom: Hawker Hurricanes standing outside the Morris Motors' factory after being repaired.

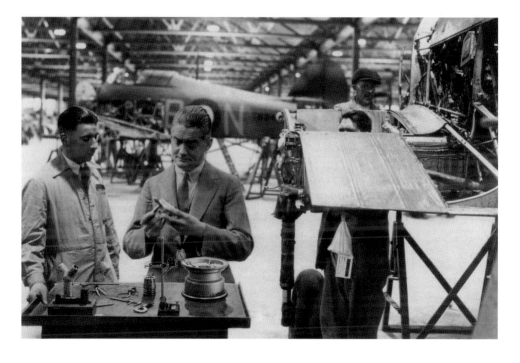

each week. The unit also carried out immediate repairs for pilots who flew their damaged aeroplanes to the airfield adjacent to the Cowley factory and 'waited for them to be repaired while sleeping, exhausted, in accommodation that [Lord] Nuffield provided for them'.[1]

Between July and December 1940, when the Battle of Britain was being fought over southern England, the CRO repaired 4,196 aircraft, all of which had been seriously damaged. From an economic point of view the average cost of each repair amounted to only one third of the price of a new aircraft and, in those crucial months, the CRO made a vital contribution to the RAF's overall fighting strength. Of all the RAF's aircraft which fought in the Battle of Britain, exclusive of 'fly-in' repairs undertaken in less than twenty-four hours, 35 per cent of them had been repaired and only 65 per cent were new. By the end of the war, the CRO had repaired over 80,000 damaged aircraft and returned them to serve in the RAF once again.

In addition to repairing aircraft, the CRU at Cowley carried out many other activities during the war, including the overhaul of Rolls-Royce Merlin engines for Lancaster bombers, the repair of a large number of tractors, used for hauling bombs around airfields, and the reconditioning of maintenance equipment belonging to the RAF. Before the D-Day invasion, the unit became engaged in fitting bomb racks to Spitfires and it also prepared many Airspeed Horsa gliders for the USAAF.

To augment the CRO's work, the Nuffield Organization staffed and operated three Repairable Equipment Depots (REDs), the largest being No. 1 housed in the building of the British Industries Fair at Castle Bromwich, in Birmingham, which had about 8,000 employees. Component parts from salvaged aircraft were taken to the REDs where they were sorted, classified, repaired and then despatched to the CRUs or to the RAF for re-use. During the war about 25 million items were recycled by the No. 1 RED, but these items did not include electrical components and instruments which were handled by the other two REDs. Due to their sometimes secretive nature, radio and signals equipment were only handled by No. 3 RED which was located in the secluded premises of a London motor dealer.

Any material which could not be recycled was sent to one of two Metal and Produce Recovery Depots (MPRDs) located at Cowley and at Eaglescliffe, near Stockton-on-Tees, which had been developed by the Nuffield Organization on behalf of the Government. From its small beginning in 1940, the scrap from crashed aircraft of Cowley's No. 1 MPRD grew to occupy over 100 acres of farmland adjacent to the factory and employ a staff of 1,500 people. By the end of the war the MPRDs had melted down and reclaimed over 25,000 tons of high-grade aluminium in its furnaces, along with 70,000 tons of other urgently needed materials such as rubber, steel, plastics, textiles and non-ferrous metals.

Three days after the outbreak of war, before any formal contract had been drawn up between the Air Ministry and Morris Motors Ltd, No. 50 Maintenance Unit (MU) RAF picked up the first of the 12,000 aircraft that it handled during the war. No. 50 MU was set up at Morris Motors' factory at Cowley in collaboration with the RAF, and its purpose was to send out gangs of people to recover crashed aircraft and then take them to the CRUs, the REDs or the MPRDs. Initially, No. 50 MU, which was the only civilian MU within the RAF, was being called out to recover crashed aircraft from all over England, but later, after more MUs had been set up, the unit was confined to the south-western counties of England only.

As well as repairing aircraft, Morris Motors Ltd also became involved in their manufacture when production of the RAF's primary trainer, the de Havilland Tiger Moth, was transferred to Cowley after de Havilland's factory at Hatfield had been ordered to concentrate on making Mosquitos. By using their experience gained in the mass production of cars, Morris Motors Ltd set up a flow line to make the Tiger Moths and the first Cowley-built example emerged during April 1940. Despite concerns from some members of the aircraft industry who were sceptical about the method of its manufacture, the machine passed all its tests without difficulty, and by the end of the first week of production seventeen Tiger Moths had been made. The pace, however, soon quickened to many times the build-rate achieved before flow line methods had been introduced such that up to forty of the bi-planes were coming out of the Cowley factory each week. This was in addition to vast quantities of spare parts and sub-assemblies to keep those 'planes already delivered in flying condition.

On completion, the Tiger Moths were taken to the airfield at Cowley where final checks were made and they were then flown direct to RAF trainer squadrons. Of the 7,253 Tiger Moths built by several plants throughout the world, between September 1939 and August 1945, over 3,500 were made by Morris Motors Ltd, thereby making the firm the principal sub-contractor for the aircraft.[2]

Early in 1942, Morris Motors Ltd began the manufacture of tail units for Airspeed Horsa gliders, and later in the war the company assembled large numbers of Rolls-Royce Merlin engines for Lancaster bombers.

Tiger Moths under construction at the Morris Motors' Cowley factory.

Of the 7,253 de Havilland Tiger Moths built during the Second World War, 3,508 were made by Morris Motors Ltd at Cowley, thereby making this company the principle sub-contractor for the aircraft.

This Morris Motors'-built Tiger Moth – NL 911 – is seen having its compasses adjusted while standing on a compass base at the company's airfield, a procedure known as 'checking the compass swing'. Note that by being raised on a trestle, the Tiger Moth is in its approximate flying position and that plumb bobs are hanging from the front and rear of the aircraft, to enable accurate positioning with lines painted on the ground. NL 911 (constructor's No.86354), was one of 350 Tiger Moths delivered by Morris Motors Ltd between July 1943 and March 1944. It served with Nos 3 and 22 Elementary Flying Training Schools and was based at Upwood, Waddington and Wittering. After being taken 'off charge', NL 911 was sold on 28 March 1955, becoming G-AOAB on the Civil Register. This registration was cancelled on 15 April 1955 and the Moth was then issued with a Swedish registration, SE – CGD.

When Morris Motors Ltd took delivery of this de Havilland Leopard Moth in August 1934, the company became the first British motor manufacturer to operate a private aeroplane. The machine, which was primarily used by Morris Motors' sales director and his assistant, remained in service until Impressed as BD 140. It was badly damaged by enemy action in 1941 and subsequently scrapped.

The M.G. Car Co. Ltd of Abingdon undertook the construction of the forward section and cabin of an Armstrong Whitworth Albemarle aircraft, as shown in this photograph.

2) The M.G. Car Company Ltd, Abingdon

During July 1930, The M.G. Car Co. Ltd was registered so that it could take over the manufacturing of sports cars from The Morris Garages Ltd.

It was not until some time after the war had begun that the M.G. Car Co. Ltd became involved with aviation, when they manufactured the forward section and cabins of Armstrong Whitworth Albemarle aircraft. At the time M.G. took on this task, there were four other firms involved in making the same 'Gl unit', but these were later to drop out, leaving only M.G. involved with the project.

In addition, M.G's. Abingdon factory assembled Rolls-Royce Merlin power units for Lancaster Bombers, matching Morris Motors' output of these engines by making the same number of inboard units, and they also made many parts for aircraft including mountings for Bristol aero engines, radiator flaps for Lancasters and leading and trailing edges for Hawker Tempest wings, a job which involved hours of manual labour with fine emery cloth to make them smooth.

3) Morris Motors Ltd, Radiators Branch, Oxford

In May 1919 Lord Nuffield assisted in the formation of a business in Oxford to make vehicle radiators, which soon became known as the Osberton Radiator Co. Lord Nuffield took complete control of the business in 1923 and, by 1926, when it became a branch of Morris Motors Ltd, it had about 500 employees who made some 1,500 radiators a week.

A few weeks before war broke out, in August 1939, Radiators Branch were approached by Rolls-Royce Ltd to make radiators for their Merlin engines, fitted to Supermarine Spitfires. In conjunction with Rolls-Royce, a new design of secondary surface radiator was developed which dispersed heat more efficiently and was lighter than the earlier honeycomb Serck type. Production started during May 1940 and, with the exception of a single Mark III, all Spitfires manufactured from September 1940 were fitted with radiators made by Morris Motors Ltd, Radiators Branch. As well as those for Spitfires, radiators

With the exception of a single Mk III, all Spitfires manufactured from September 1940 were fitted with radiators made by Morris Motors Ltd, Radiators Branch, Oxford. The illustration shows a radiator for a Spitfire Mk V.

were made for Rolls-Royce Merlin engines that were installed into aircraft such as the Lancaster and Mosquito. Radiators Branch also produced the liquid intercooler fitted to Merlin engines with two-stage superchargers.

On hot summer days petrol in the fuel tanks of fighter aircraft parked on airfields could reach 80°F and within minutes of being 'scrambled' these aircraft could be flying in a rarefied atmosphere which could cause the petrol to boil. To prevent this happening, Radiators Branch developed a small heat exchanger for fitment in the fuel pipeline, thereby keeping the petrol at a safe temperature.

In order to keep an aircrew warm and to prevent guns from freezing at high altitudes, Radiators Branch became engaged in a project to duct heated air from the engine's radiator into the cockpit and gun mechanisms of aircraft. Another project occurred soon after the RAF captured a German Messerschmitt Me 109F-l fighter intact, following a belly-landing which had damaged its radiator. Piloted by Peter Pingel, a Gruppenkommandeur of J.G.26, the aircraft was forced down in July 1941. To enable the machine to be test-flown and evaluated, Radiators Branch supplied a radiator to suit the fighter which was fitted by No. 50 MU at Cowley.

In 1943, to cope with the ever-increasing demand for radiators and to harness labour where it was readily available, an entirely new and additional factory was built at Llanelli, South Wales, which Radiators Branch shared with Morris Pressings Branch. Dispersal factories were also set up to make radiators during the war at Worcester, at Cumnor, Oxfordshire, and at Hayfield Road, Oxford.

4) Wolseley Motors Ltd, Ward End, Birmingham

At the beginning of the war Wolseley stopped producing cars turning their facilities over to the manufacture of Morris Commercial six-wheeled military vehicles and Bren Gun Carriers. They also began to make mines and sinkers as well as large quantities of percussion fuses for heavy shells. Part of Wolseley's factory, including the area which had made radial aero engines, was occupied by Nuffield Mechanizations & Aero Ltd for the manufacture of tanks including their Nuffield-Liberty engines, and these activities probably caused the German Luftwaffe to target the works during the night of 9/10 April 1941 when it was bombed. The raid caused extensive roof and structural damage to the buildings and some 20 per cent of production was immediately lost.

The factory was attacked again during May 1941, and then in July 1942, when explosive incendiary bombs were used, but due to the prompt action by Wolseley's staff and the works fire brigade, the damage sustained on both these later occasions was less severe than in the first air raid.

Although Wolseley Motors Ltd was not as involved in aviation as some other factories within the Nuffield Organization during the war, they did manufacture oleo undercarriage legs for Spitfires and Lockheed hydraulic assemblies for Hurricanes, Beaufighters, Mosquitos and other aircraft. They also made wings for Airspeed Horsa gliders as well as 20mm cannon shot and armour-piercing nose caps for use in cannon that were installed in some fighter aircraft.

Production of Wolseley 10hp, Series III cars, at Wolseley's Ward End factory, in Birmingham, *c.*1938.

One of the 14,000 Bren Gun Carriers made by Wolseley Motors Ltd during the Second World War.

5) *Morris Commercial Cars Ltd, Adderley Park, Birmingham*

On 1 January 1924 Lord Nuffield bought the factory and assets of the axle and gearbox manufacturer, E.G. Wrigley & Co. Ltd of Soho, Birmingham, from the receivers – and then formed Morris Commercial Cars Ltd to make purpose-built commercial vehicles. By 1932 the manufacture of Morris-Commercials had moved to a larger factory at Adderley Park, Birmingham, which had been acquired from Wolseley Motors (1927) Ltd.

During the Second World War the Adderley Park factory was devoted to the manufacture of military vehicles, tanks, gun platforms, transmission units for torpedoes and anti-submarine weapons. The factory also made components for Rolls-Royce Merlin and Griffon aero engines.

6) *S.U. Carburetter Co. Ltd, Birmingham*

At the beginning of the last century G.H. Skinner and T.C. (Carl) Skinner developed a 'constant vacuum' carburetter and, in 1910, the S.U. Carburetter Co. Ltd (S.U. being a contraction of Skinners Union) was formed, in London, for its manufacture.

During the First World War, the company made munitions as well as carburetters for aero engines but, when the war ended, the business began to get into financial difficulties. The situation deteriorated steadily until 1926 when Carl Skinner approached Lord Nuffield and asked him to buy the business. After negotiations, during which Carl agreed to remain as its manager, Lord Nuffield bought the firm for £100,000 and immediately transferred its operations to Adderley Park, Birmingham. From 1927 all Morris cars were fitted with S.U. carburetters, which were also soon to be fitted to many vehicles made by other manufacturers and, by 1939, over 4,000 S.U. Carburetters were being made each week.

During the mid-1930s S.U. Carburetters were fitted to the radial aero engines made by Wolseley Aero Engines Ltd; an example of an S.U. A.V. 20 carburetter, as fitted to a Wolseley Scorpio, is illustrated on page 64. After Wolseley's aero engine factory had been closed in 1936, two of the Hawker Tomtits operated by the firm, G-ABOD and G-ABAX (see page 46), were then used by the S.U. for development trials.

Throughout the Second World War, the S.U. Carburetter Co. played a significant role in the aero engine industry. Collectively, they made five different types of standard model carburetters for Rolls-Royce Merlin, Vulture and Peregrine engines and for Napier Sabre and Dagger engines. In addition, S.U. also maintained a comparatively small production of carburetters and fuel pumps for motor cars and undertook development work for prototype aircraft. Such work included the development of an aero engine petrol injection system which was first fitted, for operational purposes, to the de Havilland Mosquito.

All of the RAF's Spitfires and Hurricanes which took part in the Battle of Britain during the summer of 1940 were fitted with carburetters made by S.U. at their factory in Birmingham. Realising its vital importance after Birmingham had suffered two heavy air raids in November 1940, when the S.U. factory was bombed and set on fire, the Air Ministry decided to move S.U.'s. entire plant to a new, larger factory at Shirley on the outskirts of Birmingham. It was also decided to duplicate S.U. production at the works of Riley Motors Ltd in Coventry.

In 1941, to cope with a demand for yet more production, S.U. acquired another factory at Wharfe Valley, Yorkshire, with much of its labour being recruited from the nearby woollen mills. After the war, S.U.'s manufacturing and development activities were concentrated in a factory at Wood Lane, Erdington, Birmingham.

By mounting a 40mm Bofors anti-aircraft gun onto an extended Morris–Commercial C/8 'Quad' gun tractor chassis, Morris Commercial Cars Ltd produced the C9/B, 4x4, 'Bofors Quad', as shown here. Although the first example appeared in 1941, it was some time before the authorities took an interest in the vehicle. However, production was eventually sanctioned in time for C/9Bs to be flown in gliders to France, where they were used against both aircraft and ground targets in the operations that followed the D-Day landings in June 1944. Subsequently, C9/Bs served in Italy and the Far East.

A Morris-Commercial CS2, 13/80 type Leader, new to Wolseley Motors (1927) Ltd, *c.*1934.

T. C. (Carl) Skinner.

Lord Nuffield
enjoying another
joke with two ladies
at S.U.'s factory
in Birmingham.
The ladies are
assembling S.U.
Type A.V.T.32/135
carburetters for
Rolls-Royce Merlin
engines.

A view of a Rolls-
Royce Merlin 45
engine showing an
S.U. Type A.V.T. 40
Carburetter mounted
at the base of the
supercharger unit.

7) *Riley Motors Ltd, Coventry*

After an appeal from Mr Victor Riley in 1938, when Riley Motors Ltd had got into financial difficulties and was in danger of being wound up, Lord Nuffield purchased the business for £143,000 to ensure that the enterprise which had done so much to enhance the prestige of British cars should carry on. Lord Nuffield then sold Riley Motors Ltd to Morris Motors Ltd for the nominal sum of £100, to make sure that Morris Motors incurred no ultimate loss in the transaction, and Victor Riley remained as managing director of his old firm.[3]

A few weeks after the outbreak of war, in October 1939, Riley Motors became involved with the aircraft industry when they received drawings and were asked to make the engine mountings for the Vickers Wellington bomber. The first of these mountings, which comprised 500 parts and required 250 jigs and tools to be made for their manufacture, were delivered in February 1940. Then, shortly after the Germans started to lay magnetic mines, Riley became involved with the war at sea when they helped to equip the same type of bombers with an electro-magnetic device for minesweeping.

Towards the end of 1940, Riley was asked to urgently 'tool up' for the complete manufacture of the retractable undercarriage, port and starboard, for the Bristol Beaufighter, as well as the cannon mounting and elevator trimming gear for the same aircraft. They also made fireproof bulkheads and engine sub-frames for Lancaster bombers.

To expand and duplicate the work already being undertaken by the S.U. Carburetter Co. in Birmingham, Riley set up a 'shadow factory' at their plant, during the early part of 1941. They also set up a shadow factory of their own, to make carburettors – in a shoe factory at Barwell in Leicestershire, about 15 miles from Coventry. Altogether Riley made nine different models of carburetter for aircraft during the war, seven of which were S.U. and two Bendix Stromberg.

8) *Morris Motors Ltd, Engines Branch, Courthouse Green, Coventry*

Construction of the Courthouse Green factory started in 1928 when a foundry was established. The factory, which was built on a green-field site, expanded and took over engine production from Wolseley Motors Ltd in 1934 and from Morris Motors' factory at Gosford Street, Coventry in 1938.

Before the Second World War the Courthouse Green factory had turned out over 3,000 engines a week for cars and light vans. Throughout the war, the factory was working flat-out making engines for fire pumps, ambulances, military vehicles, lifeboats and tanks, as well as making component parts for aero engines and for Rotol variable pitch airscrews, which were fitted to both fighter and bomber aircraft.

The Courthouse Green factory suffered extensive damage during a heavy air raid on Coventry in 1940, when a German parachute mine landed between the factory's foundry and machine shops. Members of a bomb disposal squad who were trying to diffuse the mine managed to take cover just before it exploded, causing even more damage to the factory.

The air raid created a great deal of dismay, not least for Rotol, as the Courthouse Green factory was responsible for making about half of all the components for their airscrews. Nevertheless, manufacture of these items restarted within six weeks of the raid, even though some of the workforce, who had already toiled hard to restore the factory, were having to work at their machines in the open air in bitterly cold weather as much of the factory's roof had been blown off and had still not been replaced.

Left: Victor Riley.

Middle: The retractable undercarriage fitted to Bristol Beaufighters was one of many jobs tackled by Riley Motors Ltd, Coventry.

Bottom: Production of Rolls-Royce Meteor tank engines, which are seen here under test, commenced at Morris Motors Ltd, Engines Branch, Courthouse Green, Coventry, in 1943.

Right: Lancelot Pratt.

Below: An Airspeed Horsa Glider being hauled into the air by an Armstrong Whitworth Albemarle aircraft.

9) Morris Motors Ltd, Bodies Branch, Coventry

In 1876 Edward Hollick purchased a coach-building business at Quinton Road, Coventry, and when he decided to merge with another coach-building company, owned by his son-in-law Lancelot Pratt, the business became known as Hollick & Pratt Ltd. Lord Nuffield purchased Hollick & Pratt Ltd in 1923 and Lancelot Pratt not only continued to control his 'old' business but also became Lord Nuffield's deputy. When Hollick & Pratt Ltd was absorbed by Morris Motors Ltd in 1926, it became Morris Motors Ltd, Bodies Branch.

Although Morris Motors' Bodies Branch was kept busy making bodies for military vehicles throughout the Second World War, the business also made 500,000 'Jerry cans', as well as shell carriers and ailerons for Airspeed Horsa gliders. Towards the end of the war the factory became involved in modernising the interior of Armstrong Whitworth Albemarle aircraft

B) POST-WAR DEVELOPMENTS

1) *Taylorcraft Aeroplanes (England) Ltd*

A few days after the signing of 'The Instrument of Surrender' on 4 May 1945, thereby ending the Second World War in Europe, Taylorcraft Aeroplanes (England) Ltd of Thurmaston, Leicester (later renamed the Auster Aircraft Ltd) approached the Nuffield Organization and asked them to consider making a Franklin air-cooled aero engine under licence, to replace the 130hp Lycoming then being fitted to their Auster light aircraft. The proposed four-cylinder engine, type 4AL-225, had a capacity of 225cu. in and a dry weight of 230lb, equipped with magneto, carburetter, generator, propeller hub assembly and so on.

The project was investigated by Morris Motors Ltd, Engines Branch, Coventry, but the company was unable to confirm that the design and building of prototypes could be undertaken due to the limited number of technical staff available. Although this situation was probably true, bearing in mind the situation within British industry immediately after the war, some difficulties seem to have arisen in the negotiations between Taylorcraft, the Franklin Air Cooled Motors Corporation of Syracuse, New York, and Morris Motors Ltd, so the venture failed to get beyond the discussion stage.

The Nuffield Flat-Four, 100hp air-cooled aero engine.

2) The Nuffield Aero Engine

During the summer of 1945, Taylorcraft Aeroplanes (England) Ltd were given permission to import 100, 75hp, 'Continental' aero engines from the USA, for fitment into their Auster 'J2' Arrow light aircraft, because there was no other source of suitable engines available.

At this time, the Government was anxious for British companies to export products rather than import them so, to 'remove the necessity of spending dollars to procure engines … from the States',[4] the Ministry of Aircraft Production informed the Nuffield Organization of a requirement for an air-cooled, horizontally opposed, flat four aero engine for light aircraft, in two sizes of 75hp and 100hp. When the Nuffield Organization agreed to develop such an engine as a private venture with no government subsidy, it seemed Lord Nuffield's interest in manufacturing aero engines was about to be rekindled. The job was given to Morris Motors Ltd, Engines Branch, at Coventry, who announced in October 1946 that a 'Nuffield 100hp Aero Engine' had been designed and that prototypes were about to be constructed, with the following specification:

Type and no. of cylinders	Horizontally opposed, flat four
Cooling	Air
Diameter of cylinder bores	4.375in
Length of stroke	3.875in
Litres capacity	3.82
Valves	Overhead, operated by push rods and rockers
Take off power output	100bhp at 2,600rpm
Designed cruising power output	70bhp at 2,300rpm
Compression ratio	6.3:1
Carburation	Single up-draught carburetter with manual altitude control (automatic operation optional) Fuel injection system contemplated
Fuel requirement	72 octane
Fuel consumption at maximum power	6 gallons per hour (estimated)
Fuel consumption cruising	4 to 4.5 gallons per hour (estimated)

Ignition	Dual Rotax, type NSF4-4. Two spark plugs per cylinder
Lubrication	Gear type oil pump with suction filter and full flow pressure filter. No separate oil pipes, all oil ways are drilled
Starter	Integral, pre-engaged, electric starter with double reduction
Generator	12 volt, belt driven
Air screw	Direct driven. The crankshaft end thrust is taken in both directions so that either a tractor or pusher airscrew may be employed.
Overall length	29in
Overall width	33¼in
Overall height	22½in less carburetter. (26½in including carburetter)
Weight, less accessories	205lb (estimated)

Provision is made for the fitment of an air compressor, twin diaphragm fuel pumps, vacuum pump and twin tachometers.

The first Nuffield 100hp Aero Engine was due to be completed by the middle of August 1947, and there was a suggestion that this engine would be exhibited at the Society of British Aircraft Constructors show which was held at Radlett during the following month. However, the engine did not, apparently, appear and the project was abandoned.

Notes

1   Minns F.J., p.191.
2   See Bramson & Birch, pp.107, 211.
3   Andrews and Brunner, pp.217, 218.
4   Letter from the Ministry of Aircraft Production to the Nuffield Organization, 21 September 1945.

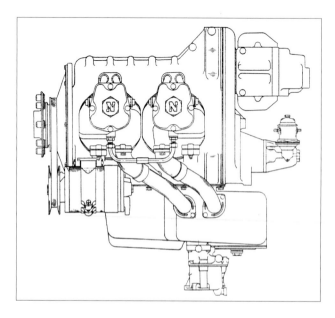

Left and opposite page: Views of the Nuffield Flat-Four, 100hp aero engine.

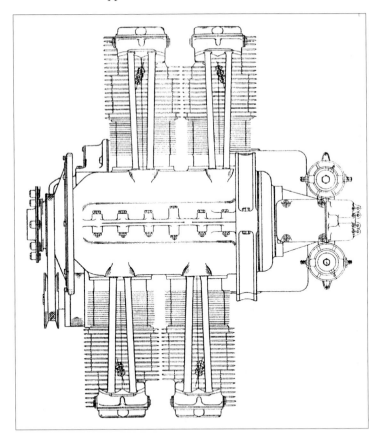

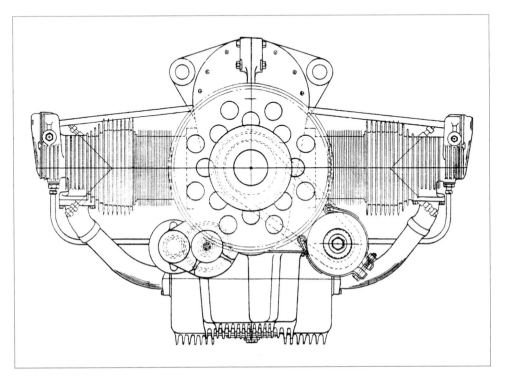

APPENDIX 2

A) AERO ENGINES ON DISPLAY AT THE BRITISH AIRCRAFT SHOW, HELD AT OLYMPIA, LONDON, JULY 1929

Maker	Type	Rated power	Capacity litres	No. of cyls. and arrangement	Cooling	Dry wt. lb
United Kingdom						
A.B.C. Motors Ltd	Scorpion MkII.	34hp	1.5	2H.O.	Air	109
	Hornet	75hp	3.99	4H.O.	Air	225
A.D.C. Aircraft Ltd	Nimbus	300hp	20.7	6I. L.	Water	670
	Air six	275hp	16.9	6I. L.	Water	620
Armstrong Siddeley Motors Ltd	Leopard	800hp	48.65	14R	Air	1,650
	Jaguar	460hp	24.8	14R	Air	890
	Lynx	215hp	12.4	7R	Air	505
	Mongoose	150hp	8.86	5R	Air	365
	Genet Major	100hp	5.23	5R	Air	250
	Genet	80hp	4.12	5R	Air	210
Bristol Aeroplane Co. Ltd	Jupiter VI F.H.	420hp	28.7	9R	Air	750
	Jupiter VI F.M.	465hp	28.7	9R	Air	750
	Jupiter VI FL.	445hp	28.7	9R	Air	750
	Jupiter VII F.	500hp	28.7	9R	Air	790
	Jupiter VIII F.	460hp	28.7	9R	Air	900
	Jupiter IX F.	515hp	28.7	9R	Air	900
	Jupiter XI F.	590hp	28.7	9R	Air	900
	Neptune I	290hp	19.3	7R	Air	610
	Titan II	205hp	13.8	5R	Air	500
Cirrus Aero Engines Ltd	Mk.III	85hp	4.94	4I.L.	Air	285
	Hermes	100hp	5.71	4I.L.	Air	310
de Havilland Aircraft Co. Ltd	Gipsy	85hp	5.23	4I.L.	Air	285
D. Napier & Sons Ltd	Lion V	450hp	22.3	12B.A.	Water	950
	Lion VII	800hp	22.3	12B.A.	Water	995
	Lion XI	530hp	22.3	12B.A.	Water	930
Pobjoy Airmotors Ltd	Type P1	60hp	2.46	7R	Air	115
Redrup Lever Engine Syndicate	Redrup	85hp	4.98	7Ax	Air	175
Rolls-Royce Ltd	F.XI A	490hp	21.2	12V	Water	865
	F.XI B	480hp	21.2	12V	Water	865
	F.XII A	490hp	21.2	12V	Water	865
	F.XII B	480hp	21.2	12V	Water	865

	F.XI S	480hp	21.2	12V	Water	900
	F.XI MS	525hp	21.2	12V	Water	900
	H.X.M.S.	825hp	33.3	12V	Water	1,460
Sunbeam Motor Car Co. Ltd	Sikh	1,000hp	67.64	12V	Water	2,760
P.1. Compression	Ignition	100hp	8.82	6I.L.	Water	435

Czechoslovakia

J.Walter & Co.	Vega I	85hp	5.15	5R	Air	226
	Venus I	100hp	7.3	7R	Air	293
	Mars I	140hp	9.4	9R	Air	350
	Castor	240hp	17.0	7R	Air	550

France

Hispano -Suiza	Type 6 Pa	100hp	7.9	6I.L.	Water	374
	Type 12 Hbr	500hp	27.7	12V	Water	1,030
	Type 12 Nb	650hp	36.0	12V	Water	1,030
H. & M. Farman	Type 18 WI	600hp	21.4	18I.B.A.	Water	930
	Type 9 Ea	250hp	11.2	9R	Air	536
Societe Lorraine	Type 5 Pb	110hp	8.16	5R	Air	332
	Type 7 Mb	230hp	5.1	7R	Air	615
	Type 12 Ed	450hp	24.4	12B.A.	Water	910
	Type 48.5	600hp	31.7	12B.A.	Water	1,020
	Type 18 Kd	650hp	36.7	18B.A.	Water	1,320
Renault	Type 12 Kh.	570hp	30.5	12V	Water	1,165
	Type 12 Kg	550hp	30.5	12V	Water	1,040
	Type 12 Jo	500hp	25.0	12V	Water	890
	Type 12 Ja	450hp	25.0	12V	Water	815
	–	250hp	16.5	9R	Air	550
	–	80hp	5.82	4I.L.	Air	319
Salmson	Type 18 AB	500hp	39.8	18D. R.	Air	990
	Type 9 AB	230hp	18.7	9R	Air	585
	Type 9 AC	120hp	9.2	9R	Air	373
	Type 9 AD	40hp	3.65	9R	Air	154
	Type 7 AC	95hp	7.15	7R	Air	286
	Type 5 AC	60hp	5.1	5R	Air	242

Italy

Colombo	Type S 53	85hp	5.71	4I.L.	Air	228
Fiat						
	Type A 25	950hp	54.5	12V	Water	1,854
	Type A 22	550hp	27.9	12V	Water	1,004

	Type A 50	80hp	6.59	7R	Air	275
Fuscaldo	–	90hp	5.34	7R	Air	297
Isotta-Fraschini	Asso R.I.	1,000hp	57.2	18B.A.	Water	1,768
	Asso R.I.	500hp	27.7	12V	Water	925
	Asso Caccia	400hp	20.6	12V	Air	695

Germany

Argus	Type A58	80hp	6.33	4I.L.I.	Air	247
Mercedes–Benz	Type F2	800hp	53.9	12V	Water	1,800
	Type 7502	20hp	0.884	2H.O.	Air	105

Switzerland

Statax	Type 29 B	40hp	2.34	7A.Rt.	Air	116

Explanation of abbreviations:

A.Rt = Axial rotary
Ax = Axial
B.A. = Broad arrow
D.R. = Duplex radial
H.O. = Horizontal opposed

I.B.A. = Inverted broad arrow
I.L. = In line
I.L.I. = Inverted in line
R = Radial
V = 'V' formation

APPENDIX 3

BRITISH AERO ENGINES OF 100 TO 600HP THAT COMPETED WITH WOLSELEY AERO ENGINES IN 1936

Manufacturer	Type	Capacity litres	Normal output at rated altitude BHP	No. of cylinders and arrangement	Cooling	Dry Wt. Lb.
Armstrong Siddeley Motors Ltd.	Genet Major Ia	8.2	150	7R	Air	327
	Genet Major IV	8.2	160	7R	Air	367
	Lynx IV C	12.4	215	7R	Air	515
	Cheetah V	13.65	275	7R	Air	566
	Cheetah IX	13.65	310	7R	Air	635
	Cheetah IX (V.P.)	13.65	335	7R	Air	635
	Serval V	17.7	340	10R	Air	730
	Jaguar VI C	24.8	460	14R	Air	910
	Panther VII	27.3	560	14R	Air	1,045
Bristol Aeroplane Co. Ltd	Civil-rated Aquila	–	420	9R	Air	795
Cirrus-Hermes Engineering Co. Ltd.	Major Mk.II	–	135	4I.L.	Air	–

de Havilland Aircraft Co. Ltd	Gipsy Major	6.12	120	4I.L.	Air	300
	Gipsy Six Series I	9.19	185	6I.L.	Air	468
	Gipsy Six Series II	-	185	6I.L.	Air	469
Rolls-Royce Ltd	Kestrel X, XI and XII	21.8	570	12V	Water	900
Villiers & Hay Development Co.	Maya	-	120	4I.L.	Air	275

Definition of abbreviations:

R = Radial   I.L. = In Line   V = 'V' formation

APPENDIX 4

BRITISH AERO ENGINES, 600HP AND ABOVE, AVAILABLE IN 1936

Manufacturer	Type	Capacity litres	Normal output at rated altitude BHP	No. of cylinders and arrangement	Cooling	Dry Wt. Lb.
Alvis	Pelides	38.68	1,000	14R	Air	1,190
	Pelides Major	38.68	1,000	14R	Air	1,190
	Alicdes	54.25	1,300	18R	Air	1,570
	Alicdes Major	54.25	1,225	18R	Air	1,570
Armstrong Siddeley	Panther X	27.30	700	14R	Air	1,068
	Tiger IIIA	32.71	610	14R	Air	1,159
	Tiger IX (V.P.)	32.71	795	14R	Air	1,25
Bristol	Mercury VIII)	24.86	840	9R	Air	980
	Mercury IX)	-	-	--	-	-
	Mercury	24.86	750/780	9R	Air	980
	Pegasus XC	28.71	85/815	9R	Air	1,015
	Pegasus X) Pegasus XI)	28.71	10/850	9R	Air	1,005
	Pegasus XIX) Pegasus XX)	28.71	800/835	9R	Air	1,015
	Civil rated Persius II		649/665	9R	Air	1,026
	Persius VIII		670	9R	Air	1,040
Napier	Dagger II	16.85	725/755	24H	Air	1,305
	Dagger III	16.85	780/805	24H	Air	1,305
Rolls-Royce	Kestrel IV) Kestrel V)	21.28	600	12V	Water	995

Kestrel VI)						
Kestrel VII)	21.28	675		12 V	Water	955
Kestrel VIII)						
Kestrel IX)						
Kestrel XVI	21.28	690		12 V	Water	955
Merlin	27.08	– ★		12 V	Water	– ★

★ In 1936, these figures had not been released for the then newly developed Merlin

Explanation of abbreviations:

R. = Radial   H. = 'H' Formation   V. = 'V' Formation

APPENDIX 5

TEST FLIGHTS UNDERTAKEN BY HAWKER TOMTIT - G-ABOD – BETWEEN 24 AUGUST 1931 AND 12 OCTOBER 1932

Author's note

The engine described as 'Wolseley A.R.II' or 'Wolseley A.R.2' is almost certainly a seven-cylinder 'Wolseley A.R.7' (Aquarius) that was designated 'A.R.II' or 'A.R.2' to indicate the second engine built in the 'A.R.' series. This has been deduced because the details for the test flights on 31 July 1931 and 11 August 1931 describe the engine as 'Wolseley No.II' and 'Wolseley A.R.7. No. 2' respectively. Also, the details given for the test flights undertaken by G-ABOD in October 1932 show its engine as 'Wolseley A.R.9. No.5', which probably indicates the fifth engine built in the 'A.R.' series. The letters 'A.R.' are thought to stand for 'Air-cooled Radial'.

F.R.	108	109	109a	109b
Date & flight duration	24.7.31 - 1 hr	29.7.31 - 45 mins	31.7.31 - 40 mins	11.8.31 - 1 hr
Type	To 12,000 ft.	Climb	Level speeds	Climb & speeds
Engine	Wolseley A.R.II	Wolseley A.R.II	Wolseley No. II	Wolseley A.R.7 No.2
Airscrew	B.450 A.6251	B.450	B.450	B.450
Petrol	Full	Full	Full	Full
Oil	Full	Full	Full	Full
Total weight	Full oil plus petrol 1 pilot & parachute 1 passenger & parachute	Full load	Full load	Full load
Pilot	P.G.Lucas	P.G.Lucas	P.G.Lucas	P.E.G.Sayer
Passenger	-	-	-	Bagnell
Remarks		Full load Exhaust collector fitted		I.C.A.N. Exhaust collector box fitted

Cont:

F.R.	117	116	113	118
Date & flight Duration	1.9.31 - 20 mins	3.9.31 - 40 mins	8.9.31 - 1 hr	9.9.31 - 20 mins
Type	Climb	Climb & speeds	Climb	Climb & speeds
Engine	Wolseley A.R.2.	Wolseley A.R.2.	Wolseley A.R.2.	Wolseley A.R.2.
Airscrew	B.450	B.450	450	B.450
Petrol	Full	Full	Full	Full
Oil	Full	Full	Full	Full
Total load	Full load	Full load	Full load	Full load
Pilot	P.W.S. Bulman	P.E.G. Sayer	P.G. Lucas	P.E.G. Sayer
Passenger	Mr Sayer	Hayward	-	Lydall
Remarks	Aneroid in machine N.A.C.A. cowling fitted. Exhaust collector box in nose	Aneroid in machine. Stub exhaust pipes fitted. No N.A.C.A. cowling. No exhaust collector box fitted	N.A.C.A. cowling. No exhaust collector box. Exhaust stubs fitted.	I.C.A.N. Aneroid. New exhaust collector box fitted with fairing.

F.R.	114	115	123
Date & flight duration	14.9.31 - 1 hr.	16.9.31 - 1 hr 10 mins.	28.9.31 - 40 mins.
Type	Climb & speeds	Climb & speeds	Level speeds
Engine	Wolseley A.R.2	Wolseley A.R.2	Wolseley A.R.2.
Airscrew	450	450	B.450
Petrol	Full	Full	Full
Oil	Full	Full	Full
Total weight	Full load	Full load	Full load
Pilot	P.G.Lucas	P.G.Lucas	P.G. Lucas
Passenger	-	-	-
Remarks	New timing gear and bracket Exhaust box fitted with modified outlets.	Exhaust collector box fitted as stated in previous report. Exhaust heated air Intake.	I.C.A.N. No. 2000 Exhaust collector box fitted.

Cont:

Author's notes. (a) The following flight tests were undertaken after G-ABOD had been fitted with a nine cylinder 'Wolseley A.R.9' (Aries) engine.

(b) The 23 lbs of ballast in the rear locker / cockpit was probably found necessary to counteract the weight of the nine cylinder A.R.9. (When the G-ABOD was fitted with an engine described variously as 'A.R.II', 'A.R.2' and 'A.R.7, No. 2'., no ballast was apparently added.).

F.R.	163	164	166
Date & flight duration	1.9.32 - 1 hr 15 mins	1.9.32 - 1 hr 10 mins	7.9.32 - 1 hr 5 mins
Type	First flight [of A.R.9.] Partials & level	Climb & level speed	Climb & speeds
Engine	Wolseley A.R.9.	Wolseley A.R.9	Wolseley A.R.9
Airscrew	Z 700 Issue 2	Z 700 Issue 2	Z 700 Issue 2
Petrol	15 galls.	15 galls.	15 galls
Oil	2 ½ galls.	2 ½ galls.	2 ½ galls.
Total weight	1888 lbs.	1888 lbs.	1883 lbs.
Pilot	P.E.G.Sayer	P.E.G.Sayer	P.E.G. Sayer
Passenger	Daw	No passenger	Evans
Remarks	I.C.A.N. No.2214 5 lbs ballast in tail aft skid. 23 lbs. ballast in rear Locker . Forward air intake. Trim on glide tail [control] wheel full back. 48 A.S.I. Climb abandoned at 6,000 ft. owing to being in clouds. Exhaust collector fitted.	As previous flight. Further remarks. Slight gear chatter slow running. Engine rough at 1100 - 1200 revs. Slight frequency vibration at full throttle. Carburation satisfactory up to ¾ throttle; weak full throttle. Exhaust collector fitted.	I.C.A.N. No. 2214 5 lbs. ballast removed from tail. Forward air intake. 23 lbs ballast in rear cockpit. Exhaust collector fitted.

Cont:

F.R.	173	174	175	176
Date & flight duration	5.10.32 - 1 hr.	6.10.32 - 1 hr.	7.10.32 - 45 mins.	12.10.32 - 55 mins.
Type	Climb & speeds	Climb & speeds	Climb & speeds	Climb
Engine	Wolseley A.R.9. No.5	Wolseley A.R.9. No.5	Wolseley A.R.9. No.5	Wolseley A.R.9. No.5
Airscrew	Watts 2700 Issue 1.	Watts 2700 Issue 1.	Watts 2700 Issue 1.	Watts 2700 Issue 1
Petrol	15 galls.	15 galls.	15 galls.	15 galls.
Oil	2 ¾ galls.	2 ¾ galls.	2 ½ galls.	2 ½ galls.
Total weight	1905 lbs.	1883 lbs.	1855 lbs.	1878 lbs.
Pilot	P.G. Lucas	P.G. Lucas	P.E.G. Sayer	P.G. Lucas
Passenger	Mr Evans	Mr. Evans	Mr. Bland	Mr. Evans
Remarks	New airscrew fitted. Townend ring fitted. Exhaust collector Fitted.	New airscrew fitted. No Townend ring fitted. Exhaust Collector fitted. Very bumpy at 2,000 ft.	I.C.A.N. No.2214. No exhaust collector box. Long stub pipes to enable Townend ring to be fitted. New forward air intake is fitted with Townend ring. Fumes bad in rear cockpit with stub pipes. Machine flies slightly left wing low.	I.C.A.N. No. HR 14 Townend ring fitted. Exhaust stubs fitted. Considerable cumulus clouds at 5,000 ft.

Explanation of abbreviations:

N.A.C.A. = National Advisory Committee for Aeronautics.
I.C.A.N. = International Council of Air Navigation
A.S.I. = Air Speed Indicator

APPENDIX 6

COMPETITORS IN THE KING'S CUP AIR RACE, JULY 1933

No.	Registration	Entrant	Pilot	Aircraft and (Engine)
1	G-AAYA	Lady Bailey	Lady Bailey	Puss Moth (Gispy Major)
2	G-ABDF	E.W. Hart	Flt-Lt A. Hattersley	Puss Moth (Gipsy III)
3	G- ABLS	E. Gandar-Dower	A.C.S. Irwin	Puss Moth (Gipsy III)
4	G-ABMD	Mrs Doris Sale	A.M. Diamant	Puss Moth (Gipsy III)
5	G-ABVE	C.G. Grey	H.H. Leech	Arrow Active (Gipsy III)
6	G-ACGL	A. Henshaw	A. Henshaw`	Compor Swift (Pobjoy)
7	G-ABIF	T.C. Sanders	T.C. Sanders	Martlet (Genet II)
8	G-ABOD	Sir William Morris (Lord Nuffield)	Flt-Lt P.E.G. Sayer	Hawker Tomtit (Wolseley A.R.9)
9	G-ABAX	Sir William Morris (Lord Nuffield)	Flt-Lt P.W.S. Bulman	Hawker Tomtit (Wolseley A.R.9)

10	G-AASI	Sir William Morris (Lord Nuffield)	G.E. Lowdell	Hawker Tomtit (Wolseley A.R.9
11	G-ACHA	Lt-Cm. Leake, R.N.	E.W. Percival	Percival Gull (Napier Javelin)
12	G-ACEG	Col. L.A. Strange	Col. L.A. Strange	Spartan Clipper (Pobjoy)
14	G-ACHJ	Wg Cdr H. Probyn	Wg Cdr H. Propyn	Miles Hawke (Cirrus III)
15	G-ABVW	L. Lipton	L. Lipton	Moth (Gipsy III)
16	G-ABLG	W.L. Runciman	W.L. Runciman	Puss Moth (Gipsy III)
17	G-ACGR	Sir Philip Sassoon	G.R.A. Elsmie	Percival Gull (Napier Javelin)
18	G-ABIX	Woolf Barnato	Flt-Lt E.A. Healey	Arrow Active (Hermes IIb)
19	G-AAVT	C.S. Napier	C.S. Napier	Hendy 302 (Hermes IV)
20	G-ACGI	Flt-Lt H. Schofield	Flt-Lt H. Schofield	Monospar (Pobjoy)
21	G-ABWH	S.A. Sadler	W.L. Hope	Comper Swift (Gipsy III)
22	G-ACFG	Lord Wakefield	H.S. Broad	Dragon (Gipsy Major (2))
23	G-ACHD	Capt. G. de Havilland	Capt. G. de Havilland	Leopard Moth (Gipsy Major)
24	G-ACHB	A.S. Butler	Mrs Butler	Leopard Moth (Gipsy Major)
26	G-ABUU	Viscountess Hardinge	Flt-Lt E.C. Edwards	Comper Swift (Pobjoy)
27	G-ACBY	F.R. Walker	F.R. Walker	Comper Swift (Gipsy III)
28	G-ABWW	Sir Norman Watson	Flt-Lt G. Stainforth	Comper Swift (Gipsy Major)
29	G-ACGP	AV-M.A.E. Borton	AV-M.A.E. Borton	Percival Gull (Napier Javelin)
30	G-ACHC	Sir Derwent Hall-Caine	A.J. Styran	Leopard Moth (Gipsy Major)
31	G-ABOF	M.D.L. Scott	M.D.L. Scott	Puss Moth (Gipsy III)
32	G-ACCW	Hon. R. Westerna	Hon. R. Westerna	Moth (Gipsy Major)
33	G-AAPZ	W.S. Stephenson	E.D. Ayre	Desoutter (Hermes II)
36	G-ABWE	R.O. Shuttleworth	T.N. Slack	Comper Swift (Pobjoy)
39	G-ABJR	N. Kilian	R. Bannister	Comper Swift (Pobjoy)
40	G-ABUR	HRH Prince George	Flt-Lt J. Armour	Percival Gull (Napier Javelin)
42	G-ABYW	Viscount Furness	T. Campbell Black	Puss Moth (Gipsy III)

APPENDIX 7

COMPETITORS IN THE KING'S CUP AIR RACE, JULY 1934

No.	Registration	Entrant	Pilot	Aircraft and (Engine)
1.	G-ACPH	T.A.K. Aga	T.A.K. Aga	D.H. Moth (Gipsy Major)
2.	G-ACTK	Sqd-Ldr O.W. Clapp	G.R. de Havilland	T.K.1 (Gipsy III)
3.	G-ABWW	A.H. Cook	A.H. Cook	Comper Swift (Gipsy Major)
4.	G-ACLO	A. Henshaw	A. Henshaw	D.H. Leopard Moth (Gipsy Major)
5.	G.AASI	Lord Nuffield	W.H. Sutcliffe	Hawker Tomtit (Wolseley A.R.9. Mk.1a)
6.	G-ABAX	Lord Nuffield	Wg Cdr J.W. Woodhouse	Hawker Tomtit (Wolseley A.R.9. Mk.Ia)
7.	G-ABOD	Lord Nuffield	G.E. Lowdell	Hawker Tomtit (Wolseley A.R.9. Mk.IIa)
8.	G-ACME	Sir Norman J. Watson	Flt-Lt E.A. Healey	Comper Kite (Pobjoy Niagara)
9.	G-ACSW	H.F. Broadbent	H.F. Broadbent	D.H. Fox Moth (Gipsy Major)
10.	G-ACHC	Sir Derwent Hall-Caine	T.W. Morten	D.H. Leopard Moth (Gipsy Major)
11.	G-ACOO	F.J.A. Cameron	F/O J. Beaumont	D.H. Leopard Moth (Gipsy Major)

12.	G-AAYZ	H.R.A. Edwards	H.R.A. Edwards	Southern Martlet (Gipsy I)
13.	G-ABVP	A.C.M. Jackaman	A.C.M. Jackaman	Monospar S.T.4 (Two Pobjoy R)
15.	G-ACTS	W.S.Stephenson	Flt-Lt H.M. Schofield	Monospar S.T.10 (Two Niagara)
16.	G-ACPK	E. Hicks	V.G. Parker	D.H. Leopard Moth (Gipsy Major)
17.	G-ACAH	Mrs Wise Parker	Flt-Lt H.M. David	Blackburn B2 Trainer (Hermes IVA)
18.	G-ACML	Flt-Lt R.P.P.Pope	Flt.Lt.R.P.P.Pope	Comper Swift (Pobjoy R)
19.	G-ACND	HRH Prince George	E.W. Percival	Percival Mew Gull (Gipsy Six)
20.	G-ACTE	Sir Charles Rose	Sir Charles Rose	Miles Hawke M2 (Gipsy Six)
21.	G-AAPZ	W.S. Stephenson	Flt-Lt J.B. Wilson	Desoutter Mark I (Hermes II)
22.	G-ACIX	Sir Norman J. Watson	E.H. Newman	Comper Mouse (Gipsy Major)
23.	G-ACJA	Capt. G. de Havilland	Peter J. de Havilland	D.H. Tiger Moth (Gipsy Major)
24.	G-ABLS	E.L. Gandar Dower	O. Cathcart Jones	D.H. Puss Moth (Gipsy III)
26.	G-ACGR	Sir John Kirwan	J.D. Kirwan	Percival Gull (Napier Javelin)
27.	G-AAIG	Maj. F.S. Moller	A.L.T. Nash	Hendy Hobo (Pobjoy Cataract)
28.	G-ACKN	W.R. Porter	S.W. Sparkes	D.H. Leopard Moth (Gipsy Major)
29.	G-ACUP	Miss Diana Mary Williams	Flt.-Lt H.H. Leech	Percival Gull (Gipsy Six)
30.	G-ACTA	Capt. G. de Havilland	G. de Havilland	D.H. Hornet Moth (Gipsy Major)
31.	G-ACIC	C.E. Gardner	C.E. Gardner	Monospar S.T.6. (Two Pobjoy Niagara)
32.	G-AAZE	Miss E.M. Jackaman	D. Shields	D.H. Moth (Gipsy II)
33.	G-ACPA	Lt-Com.E.W.B. Leake,	Capt.W.L. Hope	Percival Gull (Gipsy Six)
34.	G-ABVW	L. Lipton	L. Lipton	D.H. Moth (Gipsy III)
35.	G-ABZZ	S.P. Symington	S.P. Symington	Comper Swift (Pobjoy R)
36.	G-ACNC	Viscountess Wakefield	Flt-Lt N. Comper	Comper Streak (Gipsy Major)
37.	G-ACNZ	AV-M.A.E. Borton	AV-M.A.E. Borton	Airspeed Courier (Napier Rapier)
38.	G-ACHU	R.G. Cazalet	R.G. Cazalet	Monospar S.T.4 (Two Pobjoy R)
39.	G-ACPU	E.L. Gandar Dower	A.C.S. Irwin	British Klemm Eagle (Gipsy Six)
40.	G-AAVT	C.S. Napier	C.S. Napier	Hendy 302 (Hermes IV)
41.	G-ACIZ	A.L. Patterson	Mrs G. Patterson	Miles Hawke (Cirrus IIIa)
42.	G-ACTD	Capt. G.R.D. Shaw	T. Rose	Miles Hawke (Gipsy III)
43.	G-ACPM	Viscount Wakefield	Capt. H.S. Broad	D.H. Dragon Six (Two Gipsy Six)

APPENDIX 8

GOVERNMENT SUBSIDISED LIGHT AEROPLANE CLUBS

Year	No. of clubs on 31 December	No. of flying members on 31 December	Total no. of members on 31 December	No. who qualified as pilots during year:	
				'A' Licence	'B' Licence
1925	5	489	780	5	–
1926	6	616	1058	57	2
1927	10	1,245	2,187	82	–
1928	13	1,769	3,288	219	4
1929	13	2,664	4,505	334	5
1930	19	3,704	7,041	481	2
1931	22	3,384	6,585	372	3
1932	22	2,011	4,239	287	4
1933	18	2,709	5,090	354	13
1934	30	4,683	7,780	441	12
1935	41	5,968	10,541	644	10
1936	48	7,025	12,141	880	26

★ An 'A' Licence was required for private flying whereas a 'B' Licence entitled the holder to fly commercially 'for hire and reward'.

APPENDIX 9

A) CIVIL AIRCRAFT ON THE AIR MINISTRY REGISTER FOR THE CATEGORIES LISTED AS AT 31 DECEMBER IN THE YEAR SHOWN

Year	Joyriding, taxi/ miscellaneous work	Light Aeroplane Clubs	Privately Owned
1925	42	10	16
1926	53	17	37
1927	74	28	80
1928	81	44	125
1929	146	62	184
1930	148	68	333
1931	166	62	385
1932	158	70	402

1933	197	80	408
1934	190	95	478
1935	176	141	589
1936	177	191	688

B) NUMBERS OF PRIVATELY OWNED AIRCRAFT LISTED IN SEPTEMBER 1929

115	de Havilland Moths	1	Avro Avis
14	Avro Avians	1	Clarke Cheetah
6	Westland Widgeons	1	Avro Baby
6	S.E.5 A's	1	Austin Whippet
3	D.H. 53's	1	D.H.50 A
3	Fokker FVII's	1	Cierva Autogyro
2	Simmonds Spartans	1	A.N.E.C. II
2	Avro 504 K's	1	Sopwith Grasshopper
2	Westland Woodpigeons	1	S.F.S. A.L.I.
2	Klemm's	1	H.F.S.II (Gadfly)
1	Ryan Brougham	1	Junkers F.13
1	Supermarine Solent	1	Beardmore Wee Bee

APPENDIX 10

NOTABLE BRITISH MANUFACTURES OF LIGHT AIRCRAFT IN 1929

Manufacturer	Aircraft type	Make of engine and type
A.B.C. Motors Ltd	Robin	A.B.C. Scorpion
A.V.Roe & Co. Ltd	Avro Avian	Cirrus Hermes
Blackburn Aeroplane & Motor Co.Ltd	Bluebird	de Havilland Gipsy
Desoutter Aircraft Co.Ltd	Desoutter	Cirrus Hermes
de Havilland Aircraft Co. Ltd	D.H.60 Moth	de Havilland Gipsy
Glenny & Henderson	Gadfly	A.B.C. Scorpion
George Parnell & Co.	Elf	Cirrus Hermes
Simmonds Aircraft Co.	Spartan	Cirrus Mk.III
Short Bros. Ltd	Mussel	Cirrus Mk.III
Westland Aircraft Works (Petters Ltd)	Widgeon	Cirrus Mk.III or de Havilland Gipsy

APPENDIX 11

BRITISH GOVERNMENTS 1922–1945

Period		Government	Prime Minister	Air Minister
From	To			
22 Oct. 1922	22 Jan. 1924	Conservative	A. Bonar Law 22 Oct. 1922–20 May 1923 S. Baldwin 22 May 1923–22 Jan. 1924	Sir S. Hoare
22 Jan. 1924	3 Nov. 1924	Labour	R. Macdonald	Lord Thomson
4 Nov. 1924	4 Jun. 1929	Conservative	S. Baldwin	Sir S. Hoare
5 Jun. 1929	24 Aug. 1931	Labour	R. Macdonald	Lord Thomson Jun. 1929 Lord Amulree 14 Oct. 1929
24 Aug. 1931	7 Jun. 1935	National	R. Macdonald	Lord Amulree 25 Aug. 1931 M. of Londonderry 5 Nov. 1931
7 Jun. 1935	10 May 1940	National	S. Baldwin 7 Jun. 1935–28 May 1937 N. Chamberlain 28 May 1937–10 May 1940	Sir P. Cunliffe-Lister (Viscount Swinton) 7 Jun. 1935 Sir K. Wood 16 May 1938 Sir S. Hoare 3 Apr. 1940
10 May 1940	23 May 1945	Coalition	W. Churchill	Sir A. Sinclair

APPENDIX 12

PROFILES

1) Morris, William Richard. Viscount Nuffield. G.B.E., C.H., F.R.S., F.R.C.S. (1877 to 1963), industrialist and philanthropist, was born in a small terraced house at Comer Gardens, Worcester on 10 October 1877, the eldest of a family of seven children, but four died at an early age. Only William and his sisters Alice and Emily were to reach adult life. When William was aged three, the Morris family moved south so his father, Frederick, could become the bailiff at Wood Farm, Headington Quarry, near Cowley, Oxfordshire, which was owned by William's maternal grandfather.

William Morris was educated at the St James Church of England School at Cowley, where he stayed until he was aged fifteen for what was then an unusual length of time and on leaving school, he joined the Oxford Cycle Co. of 68 St Giles, Oxford, to learn the bicycle trade. Morris then became the family's main bread-winner as his father had developed asthma and was unable to continue with farm work. 'My so called apprentice-ship,' he said later, 'was a complete myth because I was never taught anything, and for that reason in nine months I said to my employer, "I wish to give you a week's notice and from then onwards I will pay my own wages." At that time I was earning 5*s* (25p) a week and I had asked for a rise to six shillings (30p) and he said I wasn't worth it and that's the reason I gave him notice. When I arrived home, my father called me the biggest fool he could think of; but it wasn't so many years afterwards that he changed his mind.'[1] With £4 as working capital, Morris set up his first workshop in a brick building at the rear of his father's house in James Street, Oxford, to repair bicycles and it was here that the first Morris vehicle was made as recalled by Morris himself:

> I was outside the house on one occasion when the Reverend Pilcher of St. Clement's, Oxford, came along and said: 'I see young man you've started in business' and I said, 'yes'. 'Well,' he said after some conversation, 'would you like to build me a bicycle?' I was so sur-prised I hardly knew what to say, but anyway I said; 'yes sir, I will build you a bicycle.'[2]

Morris then had some difficulty in finding the money to buy the parts for the bicycle but, fortunately, a neighbour, Mrs Higgs, agreed to lend him £4 and to show his everlasting appreciation he always had his shirts made, in later life, by her daughter.

By giving a good service to his customers, Morris developed a fine reputation and he soon began to assemble more bicycles to order. The business did so well that Morris could afford to rent a shop in the city and in, 1901, he advertised himself as 'W.R. Morris, Practical Cycle Maker and Repairer, 48 High Street and … James Street, Oxford. Sole maker of the celebrated Morris cycles'.[3] Riding his own machines, Morris won many cups and medals but he 'differed from most racing cyclists in that his achievements were not confined to one distance or time, and this is shown in the fact that he was once champion of Oxford (County and City), Berkshire and Buckinghamshire.'[4]

In 1902, Morris entered into a partnership with another bicycle manufacturer, Joseph Cooper, to make motor-cycles, but, within a year, the partnership failed and Morris was once again on his own. He then started repairs on motor cars and, in 1903, he formed another partnership, with a wealthy former undergraduate from Oxford University, W.L. Creyke, and a local businessman, F.G. Barton. Trading as The Oxford Automobile & Cycle Agency,

William Morris when aged about eighteen.

the business operated from premises in Oxford, Bicester and Abingdon but, once again, the partnership failed and Morris lost heavily when the agency became bankrupt in 1904. Morris then had the degradation of having to stand at an auction to buy back his own kit of tools with money he had borrowed and, having experienced two failed partnerships, he made a far reaching decision never to share control of his business again.

With characteristic determination, Morris resumed trading under his own name by taking a small loan from his bank and with help from certain suppliers, who had unshaken confidence in him. Morris continued with his cycle business until 1908 when he sold the enterprise, together with the right to manufacture the Morris motor cycle. This enabled Morris to concentrate on developing his motor car business in a premises at Longwall, known as The Oxford Garage, which he had acquired in 1902 to garage cars belonging to wealthy undergraduates. The Oxford directory then listed Morris as 'a motor car engineer and agent, and garage proprietor'. The venture grew rapidly and by 1910 a completely new garage had been built at Longwall and the company was re-named The Morris Garage. This was changed, in 1913, to The Morris Garages (W.R. Morris, Proprietor) – note that Garages is now in the plural – when further expansion brought showrooms at 36/37 Queen Street, Oxford.

By then, Morris's project for making a car was well advanced and the 8.9hp Morris Oxford, assembled from components bought-in from several suppliers, was announced in The Autocar in October, 1912. After sufficient orders and deposits had been taken, production of the Morris-Oxford started in March, 1913, in a disused Military Training College, at Cowley, under a new company called W.R.M. Motors Ltd. A second model, the Morris Cowley, built initially from many components imported from the USA, was introduced in 1915.

Unlike most other British motor manufacturers, Morris maintained a trickle of car output throughout the First World War but this was not through any lack of patriotism. As Morris's factory had limited machining capacity, being laid out for the assembly of motor cars, the authorities considered it to be unsuitable for making munitions so war work did not come automatically. Morris, therefore, struggled to maintain his business during the early years of the war and even though he secured orders for making hand grenades and for machining howitzer shell cases, W.R.M. Motors Ltd lost over £1,100 in 1915 as these orders were insufficient to replace the reduction in car output.

A Morris motorcycle.

Lord Nuffield at the wheel of a 1914 8.9hp, 'Bullnose' Morris Oxford, de Luxe model.

However, in 1916, much of Morris's factory was commandeered by the Ministry of Munitions for the assembly of mine sinkers, based on a complicated German design, and Morris was appointed 'Controller of Mine Sinker Assembly' with a salary of £1,200 per annum. Morris's production methods proved to be a huge success with his factory eventually achieving a peak output of 2,000 mine sinkers a week. For his war work, Morris was given his first public honour, the OBE.

Some eight months after the war had ended, in July 1919, the firm of Morris Motors Ltd was incorporated which, by the end of 1920, had sold just over 2,000 vehicles. Then came the slump, sales dwindled and Morris began to get into financial difficulties. In February 1921, Morris took the dramatic decision, which proved to be the turning point of his career, to cut the prices of his cars – some by nearly 20 per cent. Vehicle sales were immediately stimulated and the crisis was resolved but, of even greater significance, this courageous move was soon to generate good profits. As his borrowings were minimal, Morris was not encumbered with the excessive financial overheads endured by some other manufacturers, notably Austin and Wolseley, and he was, therefore, able to re-invest nearly all of these profits back into his own company. (Both Austin and Wolseley got into financial difficulties during the 1920s; as a result the Receivers were called into the Austin Motor Co. Ltd in 1921 and Wolseley Motors Ltd became bankrupt in 1926.) To keep pace, other manufacturers cut the prices of their cars but Morris was able to make further and successive price reductions, due to his sound financial position, and a number of rival motor firms went out of business. There were ninety-one makes of British car available on the market in 1922, but seven years later this number had dropped to forty-one.

By 1923, Morris had sufficient resources to buy the companies that made engines, bodies and radiators for his cars and in that year production from Morris Motors had risen to 20,000 vehicles to satisfy demand. Then, in 1924, Morris bought an engineering business, E.G. Wrigley & Co. Ltd, of Birmingham, from the Receivers and formed Morris Commercial Cars Ltd so that he could start the manufacture of purpose-built commercial vehicles.

Morris's financial policies were fundamental to his outstanding success and, in an interview given to the magazine *System* in 1924, he said of them:

> They are so simple that you may be inclined to smile at them. Yet I owe very much – more than I can tell – to sticking to them. In the first place, I have insisted on financing the company from the inside. I have never gone to the public for Ordinary Capital. In consequence all the directors are 'still under one hat'.

Owing to their remarkable popularity, the output of new Morris cars continued to grow rapidly such that in 1925, Morris Motors sold 55,582[5] vehicles, or over 1,000 per week, which represented 41 per cent of the Total Industry Volume. To put this achievement into perspective, Morris Motors Ltd made the equivalent of their entire output of cars for the whole of 1920 in the space of about two weeks during 1925 and with this level of production, William Morris had established himself as the dominant British vehicle manufacturer in only twelve years since making his first car.

In June 1926, a new public company, Morris Motors (1926) Ltd, was formed to take over Morris Motors Ltd, together with three other firms which were separately owned by Morris himself. Soon afterwards, £3 million, 7½ per cent, cumulative preference shares were issued, which were oversubscribed and, despite the advice of those in the 'City', Morris retained the ownership of all the Ordinary shares, with a nominal value of £2 million, thereby retaining total control of his business.

By the end of 1926, Morris had also acquired the S.U. Carburetter Co. and arranged for Morris Motors, the Budd Company of America and a merchant bank, to finance and establish the Pressed Steel Co. of Great Britain. Then, in 1927, Morris bought Wolseley Motors Ltd from the Receivers and, in that year, set up Morris Industries Ltd to act as a holding company for his personal investments.

Due to his strong financial position, Sir William Morris, as he had become in 1929, weathered the Great Depression of the early 1930s better than most other motor manufacturers, although both vehicle sales and profits dropped. In 1930, Morris formed the M.G. Car Co. Ltd, to take over the manufacture of sports cars from the Morris Garages, and in 1933 a scheme was implemented to extend and modernise Morris Motors' production facilities, at a cost of £½ million. When completed, Morris Motors became the largest and technically most advanced vehicle manufacturer in Europe, capable of making 2,000 vehicles a week, with record levels of pre-tax profit.

Despite these triumphs, Morris had some setbacks. The coal mine he bought in the Forrest of Dean during 1927, his venture into the manufacture of vehicles in France in the mid-1920s and his attempt to market a range of radial aero engines between 1933 and 1936, all proved to be unsuccessful and were wound up with large financial losses.

In 1934, Sir William Morris became a baron – Lord Nuffield, taking the name from a small village in Oxfordshire which was near to his home, and although he was elevated to a Viscount in 1938, he remained universally known by his previous title, as noted hereafter. (The name Nuffield was adopted as there was already a Lord Morris).

During 1935, Morris Motors Ltd acquired from Lord Nuffield the Wolseley and M.G companies and then in 1936, Morris Commercial Cars, Morris Industries Exports and the S.U Carburetter companies; the business later became known as The Nuffield Organization. By now the Ordinary share capital of Morris Motors Ltd consisted of 2,650,000, 5 shilling (25p) shares, all of which were owned by Lord Nuffield. On 16 October 1936, one-quarter of these Ordinary shares were offered on the London Stock Exchange at 37s 6d (£1.87½), while Lord Nuffield retained the balance himself. At the end of the day's trading, the shares closed some 4s (20p) higher which put Lord Nuffield's financial interest in the company at about £16 million. With the Morris Garages and his other interests, he now had a personal fortune of over £20 million (about £880 million at 2006 values). The period from 1920

Taken around 1937 in the nursery attached to the welfare department of Wolseley Motors Ltd, this photograph shows Lord Nuffield and his deputy Oliver Boden (second and third from the left respectively) in a humorous vein with the Wolseley's managing director, Miles Thomas (fourth from the left), while the trio were reliving their childhood.

until 1936 turned out to be Lord Nuffield's 'golden years', after which he spent an increasing amount of time on long sea voyages, except for the duration of the Second World War, in order to visit his factories and agents in Australia, New Zealand and other countries overseas.

In 1938, Lord Nuffield bought the ailing company of Riley Motors Ltd for £143,000 and then resold it to Morris Motors Ltd for the nominal sum of £100, to ensure Morris Motors Ltd did not incur a loss in the transaction. A year later, in 1939, Morris Motors produced its one millionth vehicle, the first British motor manufacturer to achieve this milestone. Lord Nuffield bought the car, a Morris Fourteen, and then gave it to the Ladies' Association of Guy's Hospital. By now, Lord Nuffield was one of the most powerful industrialists in the country and 'people clamoured at his door for donations to charity – politicians, diplomats, even Ministers of the Crown sought his favours'.[6]

It was during 1926 that Lord Nuffield began to divest his fortune into trusts, benefactions and into schemes to benefit his employees, such as the provision of club houses, sports fields, welfare programmes, medical facilities and the Nuffield Benefaction for Employees, a plan whereby hourly paid members of his workforce shared the dividend from one million stock units. During his lifetime, Nuffield gave away over £30 million and his major benefactions,[7] which concerned health, education and relief of suffering, are summarised as follows:

The Trust for Special Areas, created in 1936 with a grant of £2 million, brought new industries to areas of high unemployment.

An endowment of £2 million, in 1936, for the medical school at Oxford, made the university one of the main centres for medical research and teaching.

Nuffield Benefaction for Employees, in 1937, £2.1 million

A benefaction of £1.65 million to set up The Nuffield Trust for the Forces of the Crown, in 1939.

A gift £1.2 million to form the Nuffield Provincial Hospitals Trust, in 1939. This Trust made a grant towards the development of penicillin in 1943, and Nuffield's personal interest in penicillin continued as, in 1948, he gave £50,000 to Lincoln College for the endowment of three Penicillin Research Fellowships, so that the work could continue in Oxford.

A gift of £¼ million to the Royal Air Force Benevolent Fund in 1940.

A gift of £¼ million to the Royal College of Surgeons, in 1948, for the establishment and maintenance of a residential college.

Lord Nuffield was a generous benefactor of the Oxford hospitals, of Guy's, St .Thomas's and Great Ormond Street hospitals in London as well as hospitals in Birmingham, Coventry, Worcester and elsewhere. He showed special sympathy for the crippled in his provision for the Nuffield Orthopaedic Centre at Oxford, in the Nuffield Fund for Cripples and the Fund for orthopaedic services in Australia, New Zealand and South Africa.

A gift of £1 million in 1937 to found Nuffield College, Oxford.

A gift of £10 million to set up the Nuffield Foundation in 1943 for advancement of health, the prevention and relief of sickness, the advancement of social well-being and the care and comfort of the aged poor. Between 1943 and 1990, the Nuffield Foundation alone gave away more than £52 million and the Foundation continues to distribute its large annual income according to Lord Nuffield's wishes.

Lord Nuffield was instrumental in the founding of the British United Provident Association (BUPA) on the formation of the National Health Service in 1947, after a long association with provident societies.

Despite being nearly sixty-two years of age when the Second World War started, Lord Nuffield toiled to support the war effort and between 1939 and 1945, his organisation manufactured tanks, aircraft, military vehicles, Bofors anti-aircraft guns, torpedoes and many other

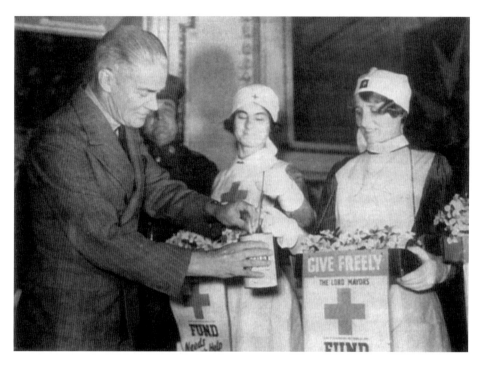

Lord Nuffield donating a cheque for £100,000 to the Red Cross Fund, c.1939.

products With the title Director-General of Maintenance, Lord Nuffield was also responsible for the setting up of the Civilian Repair Organization for the Air Ministry, which repaired some 80,000 damaged aircraft during the war and returned them to the RAF.

After the war, Lord Nuffield remained in control of his organisation but he had become aged and dogmatic. He was neither willing to accept change nor support the introduction of new models of vehicles, which caused discontent amongst his senior management. Nevertheless, Morris Motors Ltd went on produce its two millionth vehicle in October 1951 and, once again, a charitable organisation benefitted as Lord Nuffield gave the car to the National Institute for the Blind. In February 1952, the Nuffield Organization merged with the Austin Motor Co. to form the British Motor Corporation,[8] of which Lord Nuffield became the first chairman but he retired the following December, at the age of seventy-five, to become honorary president. Although Lord Nuffield continued to deal with his affairs in his office at Cowley,[9] he was no longer a dominant figure and played little part in affairs of the Corporation.

When asked, during an interview broadcast in November 1951, whether it would be possible for anyone to repeat his achievement in the building up of a huge business from scratch, Lord Nuffield explained:

> The conditions have certainly changed considerably and though it may still be possible to build a business, I would say it is impossible to expand as we were able to in the past, with taxation and restrictions as high as prevailing at present, and so many people doing as little work as possible for the highest pay in the shortest possible time and then grumbling at the high cost of living.

Lord Nuffield then predicted the demise of the British motor industry, which was being plagued by industrial disputes, when he said, 'If we don't alter our ways the foreigner will very soon beat us in the world's markets, which must result in large-scale unemployment. May I conclude by saying that if everyone in this country did an honest day's work for a good day's pay we should very soon be back to our proper place in the sun'.[10]

Noted as Britain's greatest benefactor,[11] Lord Nuffield was an uncomplicated, modest person with a strong belief in the old-fashioned virtues of hard work and patriotism. He was athletic in build and, after middle age, he took some of his recreation playing golf at Huntercombe Golf Club, which he owned, where he often enjoyed the company of friends in the medical profession. He was polite and approachable and, according to Miles Thomas, 'he had that God granted gift of making people like him.'[12] He could, however, display a quick, irritable and nervous temperament, especially when aggravated and, being an individualist, he disliked committees. Nevertheless, he had plenty of self-confidence and he had an infectious enthusiasm for things that he did.

'Lord Nuffield was scrupulously honest, kind and generous in big ways and small ways, with wide vision and…with a desire to use his wealth for the benefit of the community'.[13] His many benefactions showed that he was concerned at the sufferings of others and once told his nephew, 'it is more difficult to give money than to make it'.[14]

> A close ally of WRM [Lord Nuffield] died and unwittingly left his widow in a bad financial plight, leaving her only a small income because of his over-generosity to a Nuffield Trust. WRM personally went most carefully into her affairs and kept her in comfort and free from worry for the rest of her life. The outside world, of course, never knew of any such acts of personal kindness. There were many of them.[15]

Throughout his life, Lord Nuffield was also benevolent towards his workforce and he earned their respect by example. He had an extraordinary gift for spotting talent among his staff and many people he chose became eminent in their own right. He once said;

'when taking over any man for an executive position, the first thing I want is a loyal face. If a man isn't going to be loyal neither of us will get on together. I think perhaps I have an ability for reading faces and for that reason I have made very few mistakes in my time'.[16]

Despite having no formal training as an engineer, Lord Nuffield had an adroit mechanical expertise which he was able to combine with an innate business sense as displayed in his methods of costing and financial controls.'He was cautious, but would occasionally take a big risk when the right opportunity occurred and then get back "under cover" and restore rigid financial liquidity as soon as he could'.[17] To the benefit of his organisation, Nuffield generated much loyalty from the management of his worldwide distributor/dealer network and, having set up and managed a successful motor dealership himself, unlike the proprietors of many other vehicle manufacturers, he could encourage and negotiate with them using his intimate knowledge of their type of business.

All this, coupled with courage, flair, farsightedness and, above all, his financial policies, made Lord Nuffield one of Britain's most outstanding and successful industrialists.

Lord Nuffield's honours were as follows:[18]

In 1929 a baronet, in 1934 a baron and in 1938 Viscount Nuffield of Nuffield in the County of Oxfordshire.

1917	O.B.E.; 1941 G.B.E.
1937	Hon. Colonel 452nd H.A.A. Regiment, R.A. (T.A.)
1943	Deputy Lieutenant, Oxfordshire.
	Hon. Freeman of the Cities of Oxford, Coventry, Worcester and Cardiff and the Boroughs of Droitwich and Whitehaven.
1931	Hon. Doctor of Civil Law. Oxon.
1937	M.A. Oxon.
	Hon. Doctor of Law at the following Universities: Sydney (1938), Birmingham (1938), London (1947), Melbourne (1949) and Belfast (1950).
1952	Hon. Doctor of Science, New South Wales University of Technology.
1936	Member of the Council and in 1949 Hon. Fellow of St Peter's Hall.
1937	Hon. Fellow of Pembroke College.
1937	Albert Gold Medal, Royal Society of Arts and Commerce.
1938	Hon. Fellow of Worcester College
1939	Hon. Fellow of Nuffield College
1939	Fellow of the Royal Society
1939	Hon. Fellow, Royal Scottish Society of Arts
1940	Knight in Order of St. John of Jerusalem
1942	Hon. Medal, Royal College of Surgeons of England
1948	Hon. Fellow of the Royal College of Surgeons
1953	Hon. Fellow, Faculty of Anaesthetics of the Royal College of Surgeons, England.
1954	Albert Lasker Foundation Prize
1958	Companion of Honour

In addition, Lord Nuffield was the president of Guy's Hospital, London, and an Hon. Member of the British Medical Association, the British Orthopaedic Association, the Worshipful Society of Apothecaries, the New Zealand Society and the Hon. Company of Master Mariners,

In 1903, William Richard Morris married Elizabeth Maud Anstey; they had no children. With no son to succeed him in his life's work, Lord Nuffield is reported to have said, 'I have more money than any man can possibly want, and for what it's worth I have a title, but all that I have been dies when I die. That is my personal tragedy.'[19]

Lord Nuffield died at Nuffield Place, Huntercombe, on 22 August 1963 and after a private cremation at Headington, near to Morris Motors' factory at Cowley, his ashes were interred at the parish church in Nuffield, near Henley-on-Thames, Oxfordshire. 'At the simultaneous Memorial Services on 10th October 1963, which were held at St. Paul's Cathedral in London and at the University Church of St. Mary's in Oxford, representatives of Her Majesty the Queen, Her Majesty the Queen Mother, of the Princess Royal and of the Prime Minister, together with many notables in large congregations, attended to pay a last tribute to William Richard Morris, Viscount Nuffield.'[20]

2) Lord, Leonard Percy, Lord Lambury. K.B.E., M.I.Mech.E. (1896–1967), engineer, industrialist and farmer. Leonard Lord was born on 15 November 1896 and, at that time, his parents lived at the Hare & Hounds, Whitefriars Lane, Coventry, where his father was a Licensed Victualler. Lord was destined not only to be acknowledged to be one of the country's most respected production engineers – but he was also to play a dominant role in the British Motor Industry from the mid-1930s until he retired in 1961.

After attending the Wheatly Street Elementary School in Coventry, Lord, at the age of nine, entered the City's famous Bablake Public School in August 1906. In about 1909, after the death of his father, Lord and his mother moved to 305, Foleshill Road, Coventry, and with the loss of their breadwinner it seems that they fell on hard times. Nevertheless, due no doubt to his abilities, Lord received a grant from the Coventry Education Committee to cover all of his fees at Bablake School which enabled him to remain at the school until July 1913, when he was aged sixteen, by which time he had reached the Upper Sixth form and had received a thorough education.

Although he passed the University of London's Matriculation Examination, during his last term at Bablake School, Leonard Lord did not go up to University but, instead, undertook an apprenticeship and studied engineering at the Coventry Technical College. To keep his mother, to whom he was devoted, 'in comfort and provide her with little luxuries',[21] Lord taught evening classes at the college.

The following is a resume of Leonard Lord's early career, after he left Bablake School, Coventry, as recorded in the files of the Institute of Mechanical Engineers:

Aug. 1913–Dec. 1915.	Apprenticeship. Two years spent in the drawing office and six months in the workshops of Courtaulds Ltd., Foleshill Road, Coventry.
1914.	Passed, first class, City and Guilds of London Institute Examination in Mechanical Engineering
Dec. 1915 to 1918.	Continued apprenticeship at The Coventry Ordnance Works Ltd, Coventry, in their heavy workshops and tool rooms.
1916.	Passed, with distinction, Board of Education Higher Examination in machine construction and drawing.
1919 (two months).	Messrs Daimler Co. Ltd, Coventry, in their tool room.
1919.	Appointed General Manager at The Jig Tool and General Engineering Co. Ltd, 16 Hertford Street, Coventry.
1919.	Became a Graduate Member of the Institute of Mechanical Engineers. (Full Member in 1927).
Sept. 1920.	Appointed Chief Designer to Messrs. Holbrook and Sons, 44 Martin Street, Stratford, London; manufacturers of precision machine tools.

Leonard P. Lord.

In April 1922, Leonard Lord became the Assistant Chief Engineer at Hotchkiss et Cie., of Gosford Street, Coventry. This factory had been established during the First World War to make machine guns but, due to a shortage of work because of the end of hostilities, the management at Hotchkiss entered into an agreement with Morris Motors Ltd to copy and manufacture engines and gearboxes based on American designs. Consequently, Lord became involved in the mass production of Hotchkiss/Morris power units for fitment into 'Bullnose' Morris cars, and he was most fortunate to have worked alongside the company's chief engineer, Herbert E. Taylor, while he developed his concepts for mass and flow production. With his advanced ideas on an automated factory, about which he presented a paper to the Institution of Production Engineers in 1922, Taylor, whose work has been much underrated, inevitably inspired Lord in the techniques of mass production.

In January 1923, Lord Nuffield bought the Hotchkiss factory in Coventry and appointed Frank G. Woollard as general manager of the business, which then became known as Morris Engines Ltd (later Morris Motors Ltd, Engines Branch). Woollard was already known as an outstanding production engineer and, soon after taking up his new appointment, he promoted Lord to the position of Machine Tool Engineer with responsibility for the purchase of machine tools. 'It was [Leonard Lord's] duty, in this newly created post, to purchase suitable machines for the purpose – machines which would produce components more accurately, more rapidly and more economically than those already installed, and when the machines could not be bought, it fell on his lot to produce appropriate new designs'.[22]

In a personal assessment of Leonard Lord, Frank Woollard said,[23] 'We wanted four large, heavy duty milling machines of a type which could not be obtained either in this country or abroad; so we decided to build them to our own designs. Leonard Lord came to my office one Thursday morning to say that it was difficult to make any progress with the design in the general drawing office – we were terribly cramped for space at that time – because of the many interruptions. He proposed that he should take the job home saying "I'll have it ready for you on Tuesday at latest." On Monday afternoon he appeared with a large roll of paper which contained the complete scheme beautifully drawn in isometric projection, showing all the essential details. The machines when built were a great success. In this young man, not yet 30 years of age, I found all the qualities which go to make the ideal executive: an analytical mind coupled with a lively inventive capacity and an ability to present a case with all the implications fully considered. He was positive in outlook and prompt in action.'

With Woollard's skill in managing men and machines, coupled with new investment in buildings and equipment, the output of engines and gearboxes from the Gosford Street factory quadrupled from 300 per week in May 1923 to 1,200 per week in December 1924. Among the equipment installed to achieve this increase in output was a hand-transfer machining line, which could turn out fully machined cylinder blocks at the rate of one every four minutes, and the first automated transfer machine ever to be made for the machining of gearbox casings. These machines, which were designed by Lord, were evolved by Woollard and Taylor and they contributed to the Gosford Street factory becoming recognised as a model for all British industry. Once again, Lord was in the right place and at the right time to gain valuable experience in the techniques of mass and flow production.

Lord's abilities were soon recognised by Lord Nuffield and, following his purchase of Wolseley Motors Ltd from the Receivers in 1927, Lord was transferred to Wolseley's factory in Birmingham where he re-organised its machine shops. The speed at which Lord later got the new side-valve Morris Minor engine into production at Wolseley impressed Lord Nuffield so he asked him to re-organise Morris Motors' factory at Cowley, in order to reverse this company's decline in profits and market share. By then Lord was Wolseley's Works Manager and his response to Nuffield's offer was that he would go 'with full management control or he would prefer to stay where he was.'[24] So, after the previous incumbent, Edgar Blake, had agreed to stand aside, Leonard Lord moved down to Cowley, as managing director of Morris Motors Ltd, in April 1933.

At the age of thirty-six, Lord now had a commanding position and he immediately embarked on a £300,000 modernisation plan. By 1936, when expenditure had risen to £½ million (about £22 million at 2006 values), he had transformed Morris Motors Ltd into the largest and technically most advanced vehicle manufacturer in Europe, with the Cowley factory capable of producing 2,000 vehicles a week. To bring about economies, Lord pruned the model range of Morris cars from nine to five, and, to counter the increased competition in the small car market particularly from Ford's Model 'Y', he gave instructions for the development of a new model, the Morris Eight, which was destined to become the best selling British car of the decade. Lord had no inhibitions about following the good examples of others. The striking resemblance between the 8hp engine of the Ford Model 'Y' and that of the Morris Eight was the consequence of Claude Baily, the assistant chief designer of Morris Motors Engines Branch in Coventry, being 'asked to draw up [the Morris Eight type UB engine] from dimensions supplied by the inspection department, who had a Ford Eight engine, took it to pieces, and measured it up!'[25]

Lord's achievements at Cowley resulted in record levels of pre-tax profit for Morris Motors Ltd, along with a jump in sales from £11.4 million in 1933 to £21.1 million in 1936 – and an increase in the market share for Morris cars, from 27 per cent in 1933 to 33 per cent in 1936.

During April 1936, Leonard Lord became involved with the negotiations between the Air Ministry and Wolseley Motors Ltd, which was then owned by Morris Motors Ltd, concerning the setting up of the Shadow Factory scheme to make aero engines, on which he and Lord Nuffield had opposing views. As explained by Lord Swinton, the Air Minister of the time, '[Lord] was, and remained, a strong supporter of the plan [to establish Shadow Factories]. We thought therefore that all was plain sailing, and proceeded in consultation with the [seven motor] firms to select sites for the factories, and invited the firms to get to work, for we intended to entrust them with the whole business, the building of the factories and their equipment as well as the manufacture. We were all regretfully surprised when Lord Nuffield informed us that he would not agree to let his firm participate unless the plan was altered, and each firm manufactured a complete engine. He said that he did not believe that satisfactory engines could be produced if different firms made different parts. In vain we argued that Rolls-Royce in making their aero engines, which were second to none in the world, relied on seventy or eighty sub-contractors for a large number of parts.

Left: Frank G. Woollard.

Below: Lord Nuffield and Leonard Lord (with spectacles) seen working together in 1933, shortly after the latter had been appointed managing director of Morris Motors Ltd. At that time, Lord Nuffield was aged fifty-six and Leonard Lord was thirty-seven.

A period view of an Oxford-registered Morris Eight two-door saloon. Introduced in October 1934, the Morris Eight, which was also available as a four-door saloon in addition to tourer models and a 5cwt van, became the best-selling British car of the decade.

All the other manufacturers, no less experienced than Nuffield, and Lord himself, insisted equally strongly that the division of parts was the right way. Nuffield, however, would not agree. It would clearly have been impracticable and wrong to overrule the considered opinion of all the others; and they would not have been willing to work except in the way they thought right. Reluctantly therefore we had to leave out the [Wolseley] firm.'[26]

There is no doubt that Lord had acted against Lord Nuffield's wishes when he wrote to the Air Ministry, on 14 August 1936, and confirmed that Wolseley was definitely coming into the Shadow Factory scheme and that, in consequence, both Lord and Nuffield were in conflict. This situation, however, came to an abrupt end when, to his humiliation, Leonard Lord was obliged to resign from his position as managing director of Morris Motors Ltd on 24 August 1936, following Lord Nuffield's discovery of his indiscretion with a female member of staff at the Cowley factory. Lord Nuffield, nevertheless, was typically generous and gave Lord a 'golden handshake' of £50,000, about £2¼ million at 2006 values.

Despite their break, both Lord Nuffield and Leonard Lord retained their respect for each other and, after Lord had returned to England from a holiday in the USA, during which he studied the production facilities of several American vehicle manufacturers, their association was temporarily re-kindled when, in January 1937, Lord agreed to manage a £2 million trust fund for Lord Nuffield to aid areas of high unemployment. In this capacity, which he undertook until 17 December 1937, Lord received a salary of £416-13-4 per month (exactly £5000 p.a., about £210,000 at 2006 values), drawn from Lord Nuffield's own funds.

According to Lord Swinton; 'Lord generously offered, if [the Air Ministry] decided to have another factory built in place of the [Wolseley] one, that he would undertake its management. I very much wanted Lord in the aircraft picture, but we came to the conclusion that if he were agreeable we could use him better elsewhere, and we arranged that he should join Austins to take charge both of airframe production and of engine and assembly work which that firm was to undertake.'[27] So, with encouragement from the Air Ministry, Lord joined the Austin Motor Company of Longbridge, Birmingham, as Works Director, in February 1938, and, once again, became involved with the Air Ministry's Shadow Factory scheme, but this time working for a different motor manufacturer. Also, with his detailed knowledge of inner workings of the Nuffield Organization, Leonard Lord was determined to compete with Lord Nuffield and the pair soon became arch rivals in the manufacture of motor vehicles.[28]

Like Morris, Austin had also suffered a decline in their market share for cars, from 37 per cent in 1929 to 24 per cent in 1938, so someone with fresh ideas and new talent was urgently needed. Lord quickly made his presence felt and he soon persuaded Lord Austin to pension off a number of 'old hands', some of whom had been with Austin since his days at Wolseley. According to Stanley Edge, the co-designer of the Austin Seven, 'when [Lord] took over as Works Director it was as if a whirlwind had hit the place. Talk about a new broom. He was seen as a tyrant, a man who started turning the place upside down before he'd been there five minutes. He immediately tangled with [Ernest] Payton, Austin's second in command, and upset Haefeli, a senior designer, who found Lord giving orders to the men before he even knew who Lord was.'[29]

Within eighteen months, Lord had introduced a range of 8, 10 and 12hp cars and brought Austin back into the manufacture of commercial vehicles by launching trucks of 30 cwt to 5 tons capacity, known as the 'K' series, which were all powered by a 3½-litre six-cylinder engine; the first Austin engine to employ overhead valves. Lord had not failed to notice the popularity of Bedford trucks, so he applied his customary approach by following aspects of a good example and, as a result, the Austin 'K' series gained the nickname 'the Birmingham Bedford'.

After Lord Austin's death in 1941, Lord became the Technical Director of the Austin Motor Co. and then, in 1942, he was given the position of joint managing director, with Ernest Payton, and also that of deputy chairman. When Payton stepped down in November, 1945, Leonard Lord, who was then aged forty-nine, was appointed chairman and he, therefore, became the dominant figure in the company.

Throughout the Second World War, Lord became responsible for the production of large numbers of Austin military vehicles, ambulances and cars, as well as many other products to support the war effort including, surprisingly, the assembly of some 1,500 Morris-Commercial C8, 'Quad', gun tractors. Lord was also responsible for the control of the Air Ministry's Shadow Factory, which was located near the Longbridge plant for the manufacture of aero engines and aircraft.[30]

During the early part of 1943, Lord gave instructions for a four-cylinder engine to be developed from Austin's six-cylinder, 3½-litre truck engine after being 'asked by the War Department if he had a suitable engine for a proposed British version of the Willys Jeep.'[31] The resultant 16hp (2.2-litre) engine was installed into an pre-war Austin 12 car, thus becoming the prototype of the Austin 16, 'and Lord ran that about during the latter stages of the war.'[32] In September 1944, Austin announced its 'new' post-war model, the 16, and by planning for the change-over to peace time production before the war had ended, Lord gave Austin and Longbridge a rapid start in the manufacture of civilian vehicles as soon as peace was declared. Lord's actions 'seemed like sharp practice to some of the Morris men',[33] although there was little they could do about it. Then, 'on July 10th 1945, Lord scored a public relations success when the Austin 10, [which] had been in production throughout the war, became the first British car to be exported to America since VE day [8 May 1945]'.[34] Two and a half years later, in October 1947, Austin introduced the A40 Dorset and Devon saloons, which, with their modern full-width bodywork and new 1.2-litre four-cylinder overhead valve, engines, were largely 'responsible for Austin pulling ahead of Morris to become Britain's largest car maker in 1949',[35] no doubt to the extreme satisfaction of Leonard Lord.

After the war, Lord spent lavishly at Longbridge to update Austin's manufacturing facilities, just as he had done at Morris Motors in the 1930s. The centrepiece was a new Car Assembly Building... capable of producing 100,000 cars a year. It opened in 1951 and was claimed to be the most modern factory of its type in the world.'[36] Lord also built an exhibition hall at Longbridge, to display Austin's products, and a prestigious office block which became known as the 'Kremlin'.

On 10 October 1950, Leonard Lord telephoned Lord Nuffield on the pretext of wishing him a happy seventy-third birthday but, in truth, he wanted to sound out the possibility of a merger between the Austin Motor Co. Ltd and the Nuffield Organization. Carl Kingerlee, Lord Nuffield's private secretary, recalled the event in some detail: 'I was in my office one day. The phone rang normally. It was Len [Lord]. "Tell me, isn't it the old man's birthday today?" I said yes. "Well give him my regards." I said, "Don't be damn silly, he's in the next office, tell him yourself." "Oh, he won't talk to me." "Don't be damn silly, of course he will." I went into [Lord Nuffield's] office and said "Len Lord is on the phone." "I'm not going to talk to him," replied Lord Nuffield and I said, "but you must." Eventually the old man got up and in a minute they were back on the old friendly terms. Kingerlee seized the opportunity. After further discussions with Lord he suggested that on his way to London he should call in at Nuffield Place at about four o'clock when [Lord Nuffield] normally had tea – a favourite meal. The meeting broke the ice and Kingerlee was soon ferrying Lord through the back door [to Lord Nuffield's office] for serious discussions'[37] and Lord raised the subject of a merger.

Although Lord Nuffield 'could see that merger with Austin was the only way in which he could guarantee the survival of his organisation on a broader international level',[38] the board of the Nuffield Organization turned the proposal down. Despite this setback, '[Lord Nuffield] approached Lord [in the autumn of 1951], initially without the knowledge of the Nuffield board and an agreement was announced [on the 23rd] of November, with integrated operations starting in February 1952'.[39]

The merger between the Nuffield Organization and the Austin Motor Co. Ltd, to form the British Motor Corporation (B.M.C.), created the world's fourth largest motor manufacturer with a workforce of 42,000, which was almost as many as those employed by the six other leading British motor manufacturers put together.[40] Lord Nuffield, who was then aged seventy-five, became the chairman of the new Corporation with Leonard Lord as his deputy. This arrangement, however, was short lived as, in December 1952, Lord Nuffield stood down, to become honorary president and named Leonard Lord to succeed him as chairman and managing director. Lord was now, once again, dominant but rather than unite the two motor manufacturers into a single entity, he encouraged them to compete and be antagonistic towards each other. Consequently, the benefits of the merger were never fully realised.

According to John Thornley, sometime director and general manager of the M.G. Car Co. Ltd, 'The dreadful thing that happened at the time of the merger was a result of Austin's accounting, which was based on the theory of "kidology" - self-deception, or kidding yourself … When B.M.C. was formed, a great exhibition was created in the dungeons below the "Kremlin" administration block at Longbridge. The equivalent Nuffield and Austin components were laid out side by side, with their production prices. Of course the Austin price beat the Nuffield price all the way down the line, and the Austin parts were chosen. The engineering of a lot of the Nuffield stuff was superior *and* the prices included every damn thing. If you costed that into every Austin part you were really in the gravy. This to a very large extent contributed to the [eventual] downfall of B.M.C.'[41]

In December 1952, Leonard Lord signed an agreement with the Nissan Motor Co. of Japan for the manufacture of Austin A40s from CKD (Completely Knocked Down) kits and, four years later, with technical and mass production expertise provided by the Austin Motor Co., these cars - including their B-Series engines, were being built in Japan entirely from local content. 'Not only did [Nissan] gain the technology to build [the B-Series engine] efficiently using Austin-like automatic transfer machines, but it was also agreed they could use derivatives of that engine in vehicles Nissan designed themselves'.[42] The result of this arrangement was that 'between 1955 and 1972, Nissan powered part of their range [of vehicles] with almost 2 million B-Series derived engines in four different sizes.'[43]

After the Suez crisis, in December 1956, and the consequent rationing of petrol, there was a surge in the sale of economical 'Bubble Cars' which prompted Sir Leonard Lord, as he had become in the 1954 New Year's Honours list, to tell Alec Issigonis, B.M.C's chief designer, 'God damn these bloody awful Bubble Cars; we must drive them off the streets by designing a proper miniature car'.[44] Lord's impulsive comment resulted in the announcement of the Mini in August 1959 and, although Issigonis has been credited, quite rightly, for 'the most technically significant car in the history of the British motor industry,'[45] it should not be forgotten that it was Lord who not only sowed the seed, but also took the financial risk to develop and manufacture the Mini which was, at the time, unconventional in both design and concept.

A year before the introduction of the Mini, in 1958, the offices of chairman and managing director were separated and Lord was appointed executive chairman of the British Motor Corporation. Then, in November 1961, having spent nearly 40 years in the British motor industry, Sir Leonard Lord retired and assumed the new title of vice-president of the Corporation, Lord Nuffield still being president. For his services to the motor industry, Sir Leonard was awarded a Baronetcy and became Lord Lambury of Northfield in 1962.

Tall, bespectacled and often with a cigarette in the corner of his mouth, Lord never forgot that he went to the top of his profession from the factory floor. He was intensely proud of his humble origins and, throughout his long career in the motor industry he was tough and decisive – although he ruled by fear rather than by respect. 'He was also a man of extraordinarily complex character: ruthless yet capable of touching generosity, frequently guilty of rudeness to the point of cruelty yet sometimes capable of admitting and apologising for his mistakes. Lord was both crude in speech and manner and the victim of an inferiority complex. He detested pomp and also distrusted anything approaching sophistication in the running of a business.'[46] Lord showed little compassion with members of his staff who confronted him which often resulted in a person's immediate dismissal, sometimes to the detriment the company. Nevertheless, with his in-depth knowledge of machine tools and his brilliance as a production engineer, coupled with unflagging energy and a natural ability to solve mechanical problems, Lord could bring about a factory's re-organisation or the introduction of a new product in a remarkably short time.

For recreation Lord enjoyed painting in oils and, as a supplement to his career in the motor industry, he owned a farm near Cirencester, Gloucestershire, where he continued to live in retirement. He was well known as a breeder of Hereford cattle; one of his beef steers having been judged supreme champion at the Royal Show in 1949.

In 1921, Leonard Lord married Ethel Lily Horton; they had three daughters.

Leonard Percy Lord – Lord Lambury – died on Wednesday 13 September 1967 aged seventy.

3) Cunliffe-Lister, Philip, (formally Philip Lloyd-Greame), P.C., G.B.E., C.H., M.C., the Earl of Swinton (1884–1972), lawyer and politician, was born at East Ayton, near Scarborough. Philip Lloyd-Greame was educated at Winchester College and read law at University College, Oxford, in which subject he obtained a second class in 1906. He was called to the bar in 1908 and set up chambers in Lincoln's Inn two years later, specialising in mining law.

In 1912, Lloyd-Greame married Mary Constance Boynton. She was the granddaughter of Samuel Cunliffe-Lister (1815–1906), 'an immensely wealthy mill owner, industrialist and inventor, [who] was in 1891 created Lord Masham of Swinton, after the estate of over 20,000 acres at Masham near Ripon,'[47] which Mary Constance inherited in 1924. Twelve years before his death in 1894, Lord Masham 'executed a strict settlement of the Swinton estate with the intention of ensuring that its owner should always bear the surname of Cunliffe-Lister.'[48]

Lord Swinton.

Consequently, in accordance with the will, the Lloyd-Greames changed their name by Royal Warrant to Cunliffe-Lister, in December 1924, and they then took over ownership of the magnificent castle at Swinton Park, Masham, North Yorkshire, along with its gardens, farms, woodlands, and grouse moors.

During the First World War, Lloyd-Greame served with the King's Royal Rifle Corps and saw action in France. Serving as a brigade-major, Lloyd-Greame won a Military Cross in September 1916 for gallantry on the Somme but 'after less than five months at the front, he was struck down with crippling arthritis in both legs, no doubt brought on by the atrocious conditions of trench warfare,'[49] and was invalided home. Lloyd-Greame did not return to the trenches and in July 1917, having recovered from his condition, he was appointed as Joint Secretary to the Ministry of National Service and was created KBE in 1920, in recognition of his services.

Lloyd-Greame was elected Conservative MP for Hendon in December 1918, representing this constituency until 1935 when he received a peerage, and he was given his first Government post as permanent secretary to the Board of Trade in 1920. During the following year, he was appointed secretary of the Department of Overseas Trade and between 1922 and 1929, he held office as president of the Board of Trade in two Conservative governments. On the formation of the National Government in 1931, Sir Philip Cunliffe-Lister, as he had now become, was one of four Conservatives included in the new Cabinet, initially as president of the Board of Trade once again, but then as Secretary of State for the Colonies.

In June 1935, Cunliffe-Lister became Secretary of State for Air, in place of Lord Londonderry. Six months later, on 3 December, he had a further change of name when he accepted a peerage and assumed the titles as Viscount Swinton of Masham and Baron Masham of Ellington. As Air Minister, Swinton had the job of increasing the number of the RAF's aircraft to maintain air parity with Germany, and to assist him he formed a working relationship with Lord Weir as his unofficial adviser. Swinton's assignment not only involved a big increase in the number of squadrons, but also the expansion of the aircraft industry, the building and equipping of the Shadow Factories to augment production capacity, the ordering of new and unproved types of aircraft and enlarging training facilities to cater for the extra intake of pilots and airmen. This role was hindered by the Labour Opposition which fiercely attacked anything to do with re-armament to the extent that, after he had introduced his first supplementary Air Estimate in July, 1935, Mr Neil Maclean, who opened for the opposition said:

We are moving a reduction to show by vote as well as speech that we are determined to take exception at a time like this to the squandering of so much money upon the enlargement of the Air Service in this manner, quite needlessly as we think… we object to this country being committed to the air race that is going on. We are sick to death of all this mad talk about re-arming. Every time you come before this House asking for additional sums to help build up armaments you are betraying every woman whose husband perished in the last war.[50]

Since the Government remained opposed to taking statutory powers to direct industry involved in the expansion of the RAF, Swinton also had the additional burden of negotiating voluntary agreements but he, nevertheless, made a significant personal contribution to the implementation and subsequent successful development of the Shadow Factory scheme. Another demanding task faced by Swinton was chairmanship of the Air Defence Research Sub-Committee, one not made easier by disagreements amongst the scientists who formed part of the committee. However, he was said to be capable of understanding the recommendations of scientists and taking action on them. One instance was his firm backing for the development of radar which he considered to be 'a vital part of the whole defence system'.[51]

When Sir Thomas Inskip was appointed Minister of the Co-ordination of Defence in February 1936, Swinton found that in cases where Inskip was backed by the Prime Minister, Neville Chamberlain, he could not carry the day. To add to his predicament, Swinton had to reluctantly accept Inskip's settlement of a long running dispute between the Air Ministry and the Admiralty, concerning the transfer of the Fleet Air Arm to the Admiralty. There was also increasing discontent with the Air Ministry because of its failure to maintain parity with German air rearmament as well as parliamentary criticism about British civil aviation, both of which further added to Swinton's difficulties. His position was complicated because he was unable to reply to his opponents in the Commons face to face as he sat in the House of Lords. On several occasions, therefore, Chamberlain found it necessary to defend Swinton and after a particularly stormy debate, Chamberlain decided that his Air Minister had to be in the Commons. As a result, Swinton resigned on 13 May 1938, and thus brought a premature end to what had seemed a promising political career. It was only in 1940, when the Battle of Britain was being fought by Spitfires and Hurricanes which he had ordered, that his achievements in office began to be recognised even by Winston Churchill, who had been one his strongest critics.

Swinton re-entered Government service during the early part of the Second World War, and worked on behalf of the Ministry of Economic Affairs engaged in the pre-emptive purchasing of materials in neutral countries for war production. Then, in 1940, at Churchill's invitation, Swinton also became chairman of the Security Executive, whose purpose was to co-ordinate the activities of the various bodies involved in the battle against subversion and sabotage, and he was entrusted by the War Cabinet with personal responsibility for MI5,[52] the chief internal security agency.

In June 1942, Swinton moved overseas following his appointment as Minister Resident in West Africa, based in Accra, with instructions 'to ensure the effective co-operation in the prosecution of the war of all Services, civil and military, throughout West Africa'.[53] He returned to Britain in 1944 and became the first Minister of Civil Aviation engaged on the planning of Britain's civil aviation after the war had ended, an assignment he undertook until the general election in 1945 when the Conservatives were defeated.

In opposition Swinton was a member on the Conservative Shadow Cabinet and when the next Conservative Government was formed in 1951, he became the Chancellor of the Duchy of Lancaster and Minister of Materials, posts he combined with being the deputy leader of the House of Lords. In the following year, Swinton became Secretary of State for Commonwealth Relations, but retired from public office in 1955 when he was advanced to an earldom. He was then aged seventy-one and despite being in public service for some thirty-five years, he was not well known in the country; his triple name-change meant that he was not easily recognisable during the various phases of his career.

Swinton was a shrewd, hard-headed Yorkshire squire. 'His appearance and manner were deceptive and the unwary were apt at first sight to regard him as something akin to the Frenchman's conventional image of a dilettante English "milord". Anybody who fell into this error was quickly disabused on closer acquaintance.'[54] Swinton gained the reputation of being an effective minister and was personally interested in and knowledgeable about the topics that concerned him. He detested red tape and insisted that there should be more work done by direct contact and less writing of voluminous minutes. 'I ribaldly suggested,' he once wrote, 'a motto to hang in every room: "Bumph breeds bumph".'[55] While carrying out his duties, Swinton's manner was frequently brusque and he had a public dispute with Lord Nuffield. He was a most forceful character with a sarcastic wit and at times displayed an almost brutal lack of regard for the feelings of others. He had little public persona and no desire to cultivate one, or to ingratiate himself with public applause.[56] Nevertheless, Swinton had a prodigious memory and was brilliantly quick. He set a fierce pace and he expected those who worked with him to fall in behind; what he prized was concentrated effort, rapid assimilation of detail and economy of presentation.

> The climactic of Swinton's career was clearly his tenure of the Air Ministry from 1935 to 1938… It is hardly possible to over estimate Swinton's role as the responsible minister for three crucial years, most notably, in developing the capacity of the professional aircraft industry and in activating the Shadow industry; in determining the urgent priority to be given to the production of the advanced eight-gun fighters and the new generation of heavy bombers; in encouraging radar development and the subsequent reorganisation of fighter tactics; and, not least, in fighting for the air programme in face, particularly from 1937, of the marked reluctance of the Prime Minister and other senior members of the Cabinet. During the Second World War Swinton was able to make a number of important contributions in diverse fields but it is rather as Air Minister before the war began that he can safely claim to have been one of the architects of eventual victory.[57]

The Earl of Swinton died suddenly of a heart attack at his home at Swinton Park, Masham, North Yorkshire, on 27 July 1972.

4) Weir, William Douglas, first Viscount Weir P.C., G.C.B. (1877–1959), industrialist and public servant, was born in a flat at Albert Crescent, Glasgow, the eldest in a family of three children. William Weir was educated at Glasgow High School and at the age of sixteen he commenced an apprenticeship in his family's business, G. & J. Weir Ltd, of which he became managing director in 1902 and chairman in 1910. The company, which specialised in marine engineering and maintenance, had been set up in 1873 by his father, James (who patented several inventions including the Weir feed pump) and his uncle George.

Weir's successful work on warships, and his views on the organisation of munitions production, led to his appointment in 1914 as director of the Scottish Branch of the Ministry of Munitions. At the end of 1916, he became Controller of Aeronautical Supplies and a member of the Air Board. Weir was knighted in 1917 and, in that year, he became Director General of Aircraft Production and a member of the Air Council.

After London was bombed by German aircraft in July 1917, legislation was passed leading to the creation of the Air Ministry and the Royal Air Force. In April 1918, Weir was made a Peer to enable him to take up an appointment as Secretary of State for Air; he was sworn in the Privy Council and became Baron Weir of Eastwood, Renfrewshire. As Air Minister Weir ordered 10,700 A.B.C. Dragonfly aero engines, and while doing so, instructed manufacturers to stop making most other engine types in order to concentrate on making the Dragonfly

– even though the engine was unproven. The Dragonfly not only ran into serious development problems but it also failed to achieve its designed performance and, despite urgent modifications, only twenty-three had been delivered by the end of 1918. The signing of the Armistice in November 1918, to end the First World War, inevitably saved the RAF from the consequences of Weir's enormous error of judgement, as the development of fighter aircraft was seriously delayed.

During the early 1920s, Weir chaired advisory committees on civil aviation and the amalgamation of the common services of the navy, army and air force. He was also a member of the committee concerned with the establishment of a Ministry of Defence, and he was the most influential member of its sub-committee which preserved the independence of the Fleet Air Arm from Admiralty control.

In 1923, Weir, with the help of a Government subsidy, attempted to provide mass-produced steel houses to alleviate housing shortages and unemployment. Some 3,000 houses were built at his Cardonald factory in Scotland, but the scheme was abandoned after being fiercely opposed by the building trade which objected to the employment of 'badly trained dilutees', in what it considered its own job, and because Weir was firmly against collective bargaining even though he was prepared to employ trade unionists.

During 1924–25, Weir was chairman of a government committee which recommended the setting up of the Central Electricity Board to build a national grid and standardise frequencies. Between 1929 and 1931, Weir presided over a committee which considered the problems of main line railway electrification. He also served on committees concerned with trade and employment and Scottish hydro-electric development.

Early in the 1930s, Weir, in conjunction with his brother, Air Commodore J.G. Weir, formed a manufacturing company to develop autogiros to Cierva patents. The two brothers later built autogiros to their own designs and began the development of a 40hp, twin-cylinder, horizontally opposed engine, based on the Douglas Sprite, to power them.

When Sir Philip Cunliffe-Lister (Lord Swinton) became Secretary of State for Air in 1935, Weir was appointed as his advisor although he had neither staff, office, formal authority nor official responsibility. Nevertheless, with Weir concentrating on the industrial side, the pair became a powerful partnership and soon put into effect the system of Shadow Factories for the manufacture of aircraft and aero engines. At this time Weir was also an advisor to the government on measures for national defence, but when Swinton resigned in May 1938, he asked to be released from his work at both the Air Ministry and the committee of Imperial Defence. In 1939, Weir became Director General of Explosives at the Ministry of Supply, but

Lord Weir.

resigned in June 1941 on the appointment of Lord Beaverbrook as Minister. Then, for some months in 1942 when he was aged sixty-five, he became chairman of the Tank Board.

Weir had a cheery and vigorous personality and his standing in public affairs depended on his personal influence within a small group of highly placed men. Among his many interests Weir had been the chairman of the Anglo-Scottish Sugar Beet Corporation and a director of Lloyds Bank, Imperial Chemical Industries, International Nickel and Shell Transport and Trading. He received an honorary doctorate from Glasgow University in 1919, the Freedom of the City of London in 1957 and he was a founder member – and later president – of the Royal Scottish Automobile Club. In 1934, Weir was created a GCB and elevated to a viscountcy in June 1938.

During his lifetime, Viscount Weir accumulated considerable wealth and he became a benefactor, especially to engineering organisations. Among other benefactions, he gave £15,000 to the National Playing Fields Association in 1953.

Viscount Weir died on 2 July 1959 at his nineteenth-century mansion house set in Eastwood Park, Giffnock, Renfrewshire.

5) Sempill, Commander William Francis Forbes-, Nineteenth Lord Sempill. A.F.C., F.R.Ae.S., M.I.P.E. (1893–1965), engineer and aviator who held the courtesy title 'Master of Sempill' but was always known as Bill to his friends. Sempill was born on 24 September 1893 at Devonport, the eldest in a family of two sons and two daughters whose father was a soldier and landowner of Craigievar Castle, Aberdeen, Scotland. He was educated at Eton College and then served an engineering apprenticeship at Rolls-Royce, Derby, from 1910 to 1913. When war was declared in 1914, Sempill joined the Royal Flying Corps as an engineer second lieutenant at Farnborough and learned to fly at the Central Flying School, Upavon. He transferred to the Royal Naval Air Service as flight commander in January 1916, became squadron commander in January 1918 and wing commander a year later. He then joined the newly formed Royal Air Force as lieutenant colonel and was promoted to colonel on 1 April 1918.

Sempill visited America with the Royal Aircraft Commission of Great Britain, as technical advisor on aircraft development and production, and in 1921, he led a technical mission which assisted in the organisation and equipping of the Imperial Japanese Naval Service. Following his success in Japan, Sempill was invited to head similar commissions to Greece, Sweden, Norway, Chile, Brazil and Argentina.

On his return to England in 1924, Sempill began to promote British aviation at home and overseas. He competed in seven King's Cup Air Races, between 1924 and 1930, and in December 1925 flew from London to Dublin and back in one of the first de Havilland Moths to be built. He again flew a Moth from Land's End to John O'Groats in 1926, taking eight hours fourteen minutes for the journey and completed a tour round the coasts of the United Kingdom in a Blackburn sea plane in 1928. Piloting a de Havilland Puss Moth, G-AAVB, mounted on a pair of Short floats, Sempill set up a new record in September 1930 when he took twelve hours to travel 1,040 miles non-stop, from the Welsh Harp at Hendon to Stockholm, in the sea plane.[58]

Sempill was a great believer in airships and worked hard to raise capital to ensure British participation in transatlantic air services. In 1931, he hired the German Graf Zeppelin and made arrangements for thirty people to enjoy a twenty-four-hour cruise around England. In 1934, Sempill made another expedition by flying solo to Australia and back in a de Havilland Puss Moth, G-ABJU, and two years later, in April 1936, he flew from Croydon to Berlin in a B.A.C. Drone, G-ADUA, powered by a 23hp. Douglas Sprite engine. By covering the 570 miles in eleven hours at an average speed of 54.5mph, he established a new Class 4 record for a non-stop flight by a single-seat aircraft weighing less than 440lb.[59] (Following the death of its founder, the British Aircraft Co. [BAC] Ltd was acquired by Sempill in 1933.) Sempill's enterprise and spirit in carrying out all these missions, in the days when flying was still a novelty, caught the imagination of the public and as a result, he became quite well known.

Sempill lived an active social life around the Royal Aeronautical Society, which he joined in 1917. He was elected chairman of the society's council in 1926 and, from 1927 until 1930, he was the society's president. He lectured before the German Aeronautical Society in Berlin in 1925 and 1928. Sempill was active on the Aeronautical Research Council, the Councils of the Air League and Navy League and was sometime chairman of the London Chamber of Commerce. He was president of the British Gliding Association from 1933 to 1942, president of the Institution of Production Engineers from 1935 to 1937, president of the Institute of the Motor Industry from 1946 to 1948 and became chairman of the Institute of Advanced Motorists in 1948. At the outbreak of the Second World War, in September 1939, Sempill rejoined the Naval Air Service and retired in 1941.

Colonel the Master of Sempill succeeded his father as Lord Sempill on 28 February, 1934, and was representative peer for Scotland from 1935 to 1963. He was one of the best linguists in the House of Lords and developed many international links. Sempill was a very Scottish figure of medium height, likeable, practical and stubborn. He was the author of several books about aviation, a sound engineer and farmer, as well as being an excellent cook. He received the following honours: Air Force Cross; Order of the Crown of Italy; 3rd Order of the Rising Sun; 2nd Order of the Sacred Treasure; Special Medal of the Imperial Aero Society of Japan; Commander First Class of the Pole Star of Sweden.

Lord Sempill died in Edinburgh on Thursday 30 December 1965.

6) Wood, Sir (Howard) Kingsley, P.C., (1881–1943), lawyer and politician, was born in Hull in 1881, the son of a Wesleyan Methodist Minister. Kingsley Wood was educated at the Central Foundation Boys' School, Cowper Street, London, a Methodist institution which was near to Wesley's chapel in Finsbury where he later became a prominent Methodist. Wood served articles with a solicitor, took honours in his law finals and won the prestigious John Mackrell prize. After being admitted in 1903, he devoted himself to legal work and became a senior partner in the City firm of solicitors Messrs Kingsley Wood, Williams, Murphy and Ross, specialising in industrial insurance law.

Wood's political career began in 1911 when he was elected to the London County Council as Municipal Reform member for Woolwich. At this time he began to interest himself in matters concerning housing, insurance and the fixing of allowances for women separated from their husbands. He became the chairman, and later president, of the Faculty of Insurance in 1916. It was, however, in 1918 that Wood made his mark on national politics when he organised a memorial proposing the establishment of a Ministry of Health, which was adopted by the Prime Minister, Lloyd George, and he later received a knighthood for his services.

At the General Election of 1918 Wood was elected to serve as a Conservative member for West Woolwich, a seat he held until his death. On entering Parliament, Wood was appointed as Parliamentary Private Secretary to the first Minister of Health, Dr Christopher Addison, and later to his successor, Sir Alfred Mond.

After the Coalition government broke up in 1922, Wood's loyalty to Lloyd George prevented him taking office under Bonar Law, but when the first Labour Government gave way to a Conservative administration in 1924, Wood went back to the Ministry of Health and served Neville Chamberlain as his Parliamentary Secretary. In 1931, following a short period as Parliamentary Secretary to the president of Board of Education, Wood gained his first ministerial position when he became Postmaster-General in charge of the General Post Office, which was then a Government Department. At the end of 1933, Wood's success was rewarded when he was given a seat in the Cabinet.

After the General Election, in June 1935, Wood became the Minister of Health – a post which also included a responsibility for housing. In this position he was able to address the tasks which had always been of importance to him; notably, the provision of preventative medicine, slum clearance and the reduction of overcrowding together with the building of good, cheap housing.

Sir Kinsley Wood, left, and Lord Nuffield seen at the Air Ministry.

In February 1938, Wood's standing in his party was recognised when he was unanimously elected Grand Master of the Primrose League and three months later he was made Secretary of State for Air. Shortly before taking this office the Cabinet had approved a new programme for the expansion of the Royal Air Force when it had authorised the Air Ministry to accept as many aircraft as the British Aircraft industry could produce, up to a maximum of 12,000 machines in next two years. Wood's task was one of great importance as affairs in Europe were at a critical stage and war seemed inevitable. Although he had no previous experience in a defence department he had shown himself to be an excellent administrator and, with characteristic energy, he threw himself into the work. Always willing to listen to new ideas, and with the finesse to defuse friction, relations with the aircraft industry proved to be much better under Wood than they had been under his predecessor, Lord Swinton. Within a few days of taking office Wood made peace with Lord Nuffield, by inviting him to lunch at 10 Downing Street. As a result, Lord Nuffield agreed to set up a vast factory to mass produce Supermarine Spitfires. Lord Nuffield also accepted an invitation to set up the Civilian Repair Organization which repaired over 80,000 damaged aircraft during the Second World War, returning them to the RAF to fight another day.

During the early part of Wood's term as Air Minister, between 1938 and 1939, the production of bombers more than doubled while the number of fighters produced over the same period was three and a half times greater. The result was the gap between British and German aircraft production was closed by the time war broke out in September 1939. Having toiled ceaselessly for over two years at the Air Ministry, Wood changed places with the Lord Privy Seal, Sir Samuel Hoare, in April 1940 and then spent a short period as a Cabinet Minister without responsibility.

Following a debate in the House of Commons, on 8 and 9 May 1940 about the British defeats in Norway, it fell to Wood, as a friend and senior member of the Conservative Party, to tell Neville Chamberlain that resignation was inevitable as the Government's majority had been greatly reduced. A month later, when Winston Churchill had formed his administration, Wood became the Chancellor of the Exchequer and with it the tremendous task of finding money for a war costing an unprecedented amount. As he was no financial expert, Wood set up a consultative council to advise him and secured the services of some eminent economists. During his period in office, Wood showed his budgets, in addition to collecting money, could be used as an instrument for influencing the economic and social development of the community as a whole. He started the series of annual White Papers on the Sources of War Finance and National Income at a time when the Treasury's main objective was to finance the war with as little inflation as possible. Among other measures he introduced a system of deferred tax credits and reviewed the method for the compulsory deduction of income tax from wages and salaries. He was due to announce the results of his review in Parliament on the day he died. The publication of a White Paper, explaining the details of the scheme, now known as 'pay-as-you-earn' (PAYE), was postponed.

As a Government Minister, Wood gained the reputation of being efficient and a good organiser. He was shrewd, energetic and willing to listen to advice and he inspired loyalty among his staff. His voice was both small and high pitched and he was not an impressive speaker. He was, however, adept in criticism and exposition and he could be relied upon to take whatever decision was necessary both in Cabinet, where his influence was considerable, and in Parliament. Although he did not inspire a feeling of presence, being plump and below average height, he was nevertheless, spruce and generally popular because of his genial personality.

Sir Kingsley Wood died suddenly at his home, 12 Buckingham Palace Mansions, Westminster, London, on 21 September 1943, aged sixty-two.

Notes

1   Adeney, Martin, p.26. Morris's father, Frederick later became a clerk in his son's business.
2   Interview in 1955.
3   Andrew & Brunner, p.42.
4   Jarman, Lytton P. and Barraclough, Robin, p.16.
5   Andrews & Brunner, p.112.
6   Thomas, Sir Miles, p.202.
7   A comprehensive list of Lord Nuffield's major benefactions appears in Andrews and Brunner pp.259–263 and Minns, F.J., pp.310–312.
8   See page 175 for more details on the merger.
9   Lord Nuffield's small office, which he occupied for over forty years, has been re-created by the British Motor Industry Heritage Trust, Gaydon, complete with all its artefacts.
10 As reported in 'Teamwork, News of the Nuffield Organization', January 1952.
11 Guinness Book of Records, 1998.
12 Interview in 1977.
13 'The Nuffield I knew', by Sir John Thompson, sometime chairman of Barclays Bank. See Minns, F.J., pp.16, 19.
14 Minns, F.J., p.304.
15 'The Nuffield I knew', by Sir John Thompson, sometime chairman of Barclays Bank. See Minns, F.J., pp.16, 19.
16 Interview broadcast in 1951.
17 'The Nuffield I knew' by Sir John Thompson, see Minns, F.J., p.16.
18 See Andrews & Brunner, p.xi.
19 Minns. F.J., p.xiii.
20 Minns, F.J., p.308.
21 Thomas, Sir Miles, p.180.
22 *The Motor*, July 6 1955, p.883.
23 *The Motor*, July 6 1955, pp.883, 884.
24 Thomas, Sir Miles, p.171.
25 Wood, Jonathan, '*Wheels of Misfortune*', p.60.
26 Viscount Swinton, p.116.

27 Viscount Swinton, p.166.

28 Miles Thomas, who became Lord Nuffield's deputy and managing director of Morris Motors Ltd four years, after Lord's departure to the Austin Motor Co., 'was placed under contract which entailed that [he] should not, for a period of seven years, work for a competitive motor manufacturer. This, [he suspected] was [Lord] Nuffield's reflex to L.P. Lord's transition to a top executive position in Austin's …' See Thomas, Sir Miles, p.254.

29 Sharratt, Barney, p.49.

30 Between 1938 and 1945, the Shadow Factory at Longbridge assembled and tested 14,330 Bristol Mercury and Pegasus aero engines, in addition to making 42,185 crankshaft/airscrew shaft sub-assemblies for these engines, and built the following aircraft: 720 Stirling Bombers, over 300 Lancaster Bombers, 1,229 Fairy Battles and 300 Hurricane Fighters. The factory also made wings and components for other types of aircraft and Austin contributed 359 fuselages to Horsa Glider production.

31 Sharratt, Barney, p.57.

32 Sharratt, Barney, p.57.

33 Turner, Graham, p.92.

34 Wood, Jonathan, '*Wheels of Misfortune*', p.102. As much of their Cowley factory had been re-organised to manufacture and repair aircraft during the war, Morris Motors was unable to change over to peace time production as quickly as Austin.

35 Ibid.

36 Ibid.

37 Adeney, Martin, p.199.

38 Minns, F. John, pp.80, 81.

39 Ibid.

40 The £14 million capital of the British Motor Corporation was issued as follows: £9½ million in Preference Shares (of which £4.8 million went to Morris Motors' shareholders and £4.4 million to those of the Austin Motor Company) and £4.8 million in Ordinary Shares (of which £2.65 million went to Morris's shareholders and £2.18 to Austin's). See Andrews & Brunner, p.254.

41 Interview with *Classic and Sports Car* magazine, October 1989. See also Minns, F. John., p.82.

42 Sharratt, Barney, p.154.

43 Ibid.

44 Wood, Jonathan, '*Wheels of Misfortune*', p.136.

45 Ibid.

46 Turner, Graham, p.90.

47 Cross, J.A., p.5.

48 Cross, J.A., p.6.

49 Cross, J.A., p.8.

50 Viscount Swinton, p.118.

51 Cross, J.A., p.172.

52 Cross, J.A., p.227.

53 *The Times*, 29 July 1972.

54 *The Times*, 29 July 1972.

55 *The Times*, 29 July 1972.

56 Cross, J.A., p.292.

57 Cross, J.A., p.295.

58 Lewis, Peter, p.214.

59 Lewis, Peter, p.284.

BIBLIOGRAPHY

BOOKS

Adeney, Martin, *Nuffield a Biography*, 1993.

Andrews, P.W.S. and Brunner E., *The Life of Lord Nuffield*, 1955.

Babbington Smith, C., *Amy Johnson*, 1967.

Bingham, Victor F., *Supermarine Fighter Aircraft*, 2004.

Boughton, Terence, *British Light Aeroplane*, 1963.

Bramson & Birch, '*The Tiger Moth Story*, 1982.

Bulman, George Purvis, *The Memories of, edited and with commentary by M.C.Neale*, 2001.

Burls, G.A., *Aero Engines*, 1916.

Cross, J.A., *Lord Swinton*, 1982.

Fairfax, Ernest, *Calling All Arms* (no date.)

Gibbs-Smith, C.H., *The Rebirth of European Aviation*, 1974.

Gunston, Bill, *By Jupiter! The Life of Sir Roy Fedden*, 1978.

Jackson, Robert, *The Nuffield Story*, 1964.

Jarman, Lytton P., and Barraclough, Robin, *The Bullnose and Flatnose Morris*, 1976.

King, Peter, *The Motor Men*, 1989.

Lambert, Z.E., & Wyatt, R.J., *Lord Austin – The Man*, 1968.

Leasor, J., *Wheels to Fortune*, 1954.

Leetham, L.A., *Rearsby Recalled, Memories of an Auster Test Pilot*, 1995.

Lewis, Peter, *British Racing and Record Breaking Aircraft*, 1971.

Lumsden, Alec, *British Piston Aero-Engines and their Aircraft*, 1994.

Mason, Francis K., *Hawker Aircraft*, 1961.

Middleton, D.H., *Airspeed The Company and its Aeroplanes*, 1982.

Middleton, D., *Test Pilots*, 1985.

Minns, F. John, *Wealth Well Given*, 1994.

Montgomery Hyde, H., *British Air Policy Between the Wars*, 1976.

Nixon, St John C., *Wolseley*, 1949.

Ord-Hume, A., *British Light Aeroplanes 1920–1940*, 2000.

Painting, Norman, *The Real Wolseley: Adderley Park Works 1901–1926*, 2002.

Penrose, H., *British Aviation, Widening Horizons*, 1979.

Reader, W.J., *Architect of Air Power: The Life of the First Viscount Weir of Eastwood, 1877–1959*, 1968.

Richardson, Kenneth, *The British Motor Industry 1896–1939*, 1977.

Richie, Sebastion, *Industry and Air Power*, 1997.

Robertson, Bruce, *Spitfire – The Story of a Famous Fighter*, 1960.

Seymour, Peter J., *Morris Light Vans 1924–1934*, 1999.

Setright, L.J.K., *The Power to Fly*, 1971.

Sharratt, Barney, *Men and Motors of 'The Austin'*.

Shute, Nevil, *Slide Rule*, 1954.

Smith, Malcolm, *British Air Strategy Between the Wars*, 1984.

Swinton, Viscount, *I Remember*, 1946.

Taylor, H.A., *Airspeed Since 1931*, 1970.

Thomas, Sir Miles., *Out on a Wing*, 1964.

Turner, Graham, *The Leyland Papers*, 1971.

Wood, Jonathan, *The Motor Industry of Great Britain – Centenary Book*, 1996.
Wood, Jonathan, *MG from A to Z*, 1998.
Wood, Jonathan, *Wheels of Misfortune*, 1988.

MAGAZINES, NEWSPAPERS, GOVERNMENT PUBLICATIONS, HANDBOOKS, BROCHURES AND ANNUALS

Aero Manual (compiled by The Motor, 1909)
The Aeroplane
Aircraft Engineering
Autocar
Birmingham Gazette
British Civil Aircraft Register.
Civil Aviation Statistical and Technical Review (HM Stationery Office)
Flight
Garage and Motor Agent
Guinness Book of Records
Janes All The World Aircraft (Sampson Low, Marston and Co. Ltd)
Oxford Dictionary of National Biography (Oxford University Press, 2004)
Maintenance of Wolseley Scorpio Air-Cooled Radial Engines. Instruction Handbook issued by Wolseley Aero
   Engines Ltd Sept. 1935
Morris Owner
Motor
Motoring Illustrated
Note on the Policy of His Majesty's Government in relation to the Production of Aero-Engines. CMD 5295.
   October 1936
Practical Motorist
*Sales Brochure for Wolseley Aero Engines, c.*1936
System
Teamwork
The Times

WOLSELEY PATENTS

No.6038, accepted 13 Jan. 1909	Improvements in the drive mechanism of Aeroplanes
No.18168, accepted 7 Aug. 1913	Improvements in the Means Employed in Cooling Internal Combustion Engines of Aeroplanes and other Power-propelled Aerial Bodies
No.347552, accepted 30 April 1931	Improvements in Spring Drive or Couplings for the Transmission of Power
No. 48471, accepted 14 May 1931	Improvements in the Charge Heating and Lubricating Systems of Internal Combustion Engines
No.349364, accepted 28 May 1931	Improvements in Means for Ventilating the Crankcase of Internal Combustion Engines
No.352735, accepted 16 July 1931	Improvements in Means of Starting Internal Combustion Engines
No.352753, accepted 16 July 1931	Improvements relating to the Lubrication of Internal Combustion Engines
No.355450, accepted 27 April 1931	Improvements relating to the Master Connecting-rods of Radial Engines
No.411409, accepted 7 June 1934	Improvements relating to Tappets for the Valves of Internal Combustion Engines
No. 422408, accepted 10 Jan. 1935	Improvements relating to Tappets for the valves of Radial-Cylinder Internal Combustion Engines

INDEX

If you are interested in purchasing other books published by Tempus, or in case you have difficulty finding
any Tempus books in your local bookshop, you can also place orders directly through our website

www.tempus-publishing.com